AF316662

Growing Upward

my lifelong journey with mental health

DUSTIN PEAD

SELF-PUBLISHED © 2024
CHIEF CREATIVE CONSULTANTS, LLC
dustinpead.com

DEDICATION

To Sarah, Ethan, and Aubrey.
To mom, dad, and Noelle.

The email addresses cited in this text were current as of October 2024; unless otherwise noted.

Notes:
1. Charles Mackesy, *The Boy, the Mole, the Fox and the Horse* (Canada, HarperOne, 2019), 65

Managing Editor: A.E. Williams
Copyeditor: A.E. Williams Editorial
Proofreader: Madison Eigel
Senior Graphic Designer: Sarah Pead Creative, LLC
Cover Designer: Sarah Pead
Printer: IngramSpark

Printed in the United States of America   10 9 8 7 6 5 4 3 2 1

ISBN 979-8-2184-6565-0 (HC)
ISBN 979-8-3302-6526-8 (eBook)

First edition October 2024

CONTENTS

FOREWORD

When Dustin asked me to write the foreword for his upcoming book, there was no hesitation. Few people in this world balance incredible creativity alongside complete discipline. When I met Dustin, I knew his gifting and wiring were unlike others. His passion for his family, drive to pursue his calling, and deep empathy and compassion for people form him into one of the most incredible humans I've encountered.

Sharing my grief with Dustin in real time was very painful. As he mentions in his book, God brings the right people at the right time to help you through the most difficult moments. I am grateful to his family, and especially to him. When my brother passed away in September of 2020, Dustin was the first to call and the first to come to my house. He sat with us, grieved with us, and showed that he is not just a good friend, but my best friend.

In the years since, we've been on a journey of healing. Grief doesn't go away; it just changes. We've learned, wept, and shared life together. Although I lost my brother that day in September, I gained one right back. Dustin and I have walked through the darkest days in both personal and professional settings, and I am proud to call him my friend, co-worker, and brother.

As you'll discover in this book, Dustin's writings are anchored in transparency and vulnerability. As an author, speaker, and coach, Dustin has always prided himself on being true to who he is. As I delved into this captivating portrayal of his life, I found myself fully immersed in his world, sitting at his table, and conversing with his parents. My heart was ripped into pieces during the final chapters. Reading about the internal pain gave me a fresh and raw perspective that is not for the faint of heart.

While I never had the privilege of sitting at the table with his family while they were alive, after reading *Growing Upward*, I feel fully educated about his life and upbringing—his struggles and successes, his pain, and his joy.

Dustin's openness throughout this book evokes two simultaneous emotions: a profound empathy for a man in the process of healing, and a strong sense of hope that our own trials, challenges, and pains can and will be conquered. The tools and experiences Dustin shares in these pages will embolden each of us to fight, to seek assistance, and to triumph over the battles that rage within our minds and our lives.

So, take a step forward and accept the challenge. Join the Pead family, along with me, in learning from this powerful writing. Dustin's journey is one that many of us, whether in the public eye or hidden from view, navigate daily. If nothing else, let this book inspire you to bring to light those hidden pains and discover the healing that Dustin has found. It's a journey that will last a lifetime, but it's a journey that's worth every single second.

I think we all benefit from personal growth in our lives. Never settle, never get complacent. Pursue health, freedom, and meaningful relationships. Embrace vulnerability, be willing to change, and stay open-minded. By doing so, you can also experience the healing that Dustin has found on his journey.

Chris Comstock,
Grateful Best Friend

INTRODUCTION

I'll be honest, I never know how long introductions are supposed to be. Yes, this is my first book, thus my first introduction, but even when I'm reading, I often wonder how long does an introduction need to be anyway. I know plenty of readers who skip the introduction, and I am often guilty of that as well. I guess my attempt here is to further convince you, the reader, that this book is for you too. This book is not just some memoir for the sake of checking off a life goal, although that's certainly part of it. But if I write a book that doesn't serve people or the greater understanding of our modern world, what good is it?

With all of that said, here's my (short) introduction:

There are moments throughout our lives that define us all. Growing up in a normal home with what I assumed was a normal family with normal problems, I learned very quickly how to suppress my feelings and not be a burden to others. I was too young to know then that I was setting the table for the enemy to have a seat there. That set the path for moment after moment in my early years to let the enemy in.

Maybe you can relate, but throughout my life it has felt like one step forward, two steps back. Many triumphs, even more failures, losses, and grief would plague my life for decades. I couldn't tell you back then what I was facing was rooted in my mind and my upbringing, but I knew I loved my family, I was passionate about what I felt God had called me to, and no matter how far I ran, I couldn't outrun my thoughts, which would cripple me time and time again.

Growing up, I never thought any of my thoughts were unhealthy. I assumed, like most of us, through the lens of childhood innocence that everyone thought the way I did. I remember thinking regularly that my life and experiences are no different than anyone else's, rationalizing the abnormalities of childhood in the '80s and '90s where the drama was so regular it felt normal. Most of this book still, in a way, feels normal. But it's only through the lens of living a life with others and a close connection to my God that I realize how broken we all are.

If you have ever struggled with having your thoughts control your life rather than you being in control of your thoughts, this book is for you.

It's always been important to me to be authentic, open, and honest with how I'm feeling. It has gotten me in trouble many times, but overall, I still feel like being vulnerable is worth it. This book is a vulnerable attempt to have readers relate to the struggle that many of us still aren't comfortable addressing in ourselves.

Through over a decade of struggling therapy, reflection, learning to grieve, I believe my story will resonate with others like me. I want them to know, although their story is unique, they are not alone in this battle. They, like me, can overcome. I want to tell you my story of growing upward.

"Asking for help isn't giving up…
it's refusing to give up."

—Charlie Mackesy, *The Boy, the Mole, the Fox and the Horse*

CHAPTER ONE

CHILDHOOD INNOCENCE

My earliest memories in life are filled with smell. The smell of fresh cut grass on a summer evening. The smell of fried chicken on a Sunday afternoon. The smell of my dad's cigars and English Leather cologne permeating the air of the house and his shiny 1990 F-150 XLT with chrome American Racing wheels. Dad used to actually use his cologne, which often switched between English Leather and Stetson, to wipe down the interior of his prized truck. Maybe this was to mask the smell of stale cigars, but either way, I recall it with the fondest of sensory memories.

I remember the smell of racing fuel and corndogs on a Friday night at Southside Speedway, in Chesterfield, Virginia, where my love for stock-car racing first soared. Smells of Marlboro Lights when we visited my aunt, Betty Sue, and her family just down the road. The smell of the town next to ours where both my parents worked. It was a river town, a factory town, a blue-collar town. A town where my dad would tell countless tales of growing up in and how picturesque it used to be. A town you could smell as you crossed the small creek bridge to drive into it. It had a smell of waste, mostly due to the paper mill my father labored at for over thirty years. He would bring that smell home with him and, mixed with his musk of cigars and cheap cologne, it was so comforting to me. He said he hated the work, but I think he secretly loved it. He had great friends that we would hang out with regularly outside of the factory where he held a job that was not too difficult but worked him in shifts. 7:00 a.m. to 3:00 p.m., or daylight, was his least favorite because the bosses were around barking out orders for "no good reason." I think the 3:00 p.m. to 11:00 p.m. shift was his favorite. He could sleep in and do whatever he wanted to for most of the day before packing a cooler of beer to drink in the parking lot at the end of his shift, heading in to work as his bosses headed out. Often, when he got off those shifts he would come home, shower, and take me with him to grab a sack of greasy fast food, then come back home and watch reruns of *Jake and the Fatman*, *In the Heat of the Night*, or *The Three Stooges* before coming to bed with full bellies and fuller hearts from time spent together.

Then there was the graveyard shift, 11:00 p.m. to 7:00 a.m. He seemed to dislike this shift, and years later I would realize why. I was eighteen when I took a temp job that lasted only a week with a friend where we worked this graveyard shift at a local Lowe's, restocking and rearranging 3M products. That was the strangest and longest week of my life. It felt like one long, groggy day. I was so tired, hungry at the weirdest times, and not very pleasant to be around. This made me empathize immediately with my dad and the eggshells we had to walk on when he was working this shift while I was growing up. It brought such tension in our household. My mother quieted us down each time we got louder than a whisper. "Your dad is sleeping!" she would yell. I always wondered what would disturb dad more: us kids being kids, or my mom yelling at us to stop.

I remember the smell of getting off the school bus and noticing the windows of our 1980s tri-level wide open with scents of chili dogs and french fries being prepared by my dad, cigar in his mouth, in the kitchen, while Motown oldies music blasted.. What a time to be alive.

My sister Noelle was six years older than me. I was told, when I was little, we were tight. Always playing with each other and keeping each other entertained. I don't remember much of those days. As you'll read in a later chapter, I just remember my sister being at odds with all of us. But despite all of her flaws, she was fun to be around. Her laugh was so infectious. She snorted like a pig, but not through her nose. "The Pead Laugh," as it would become known, was a snorting in the throat, and so involuntary you'd wonder where it came from. I remember the smell of her putting Thousand Island dressing on everything that was edible and the endless Reese's Peanut Butter Cups she consumed on Friday nights, sitting on a pallet of blankets with me while we watched TGIF on ABC. I remember the smell of the kerosene heater my dad used in the garage in the winter months to keep warm while he escaped the burdens of fatherhood and husbandry. The garage was his haven. A true "man cave" long before the term ever existed. He had a wall of trucker hats at the back of the garage that spanned the entire width of his concrete palace. There was a TV in the corner, a dart board, a beer fridge, NASCAR racing memorabilia, and more cassette tapes of his favorite music than you could even count. Of course there were tools in there too, and a copy of a book that I always laughed at but never once saw him open called *How to Fix Damn Near Everything*. I'm sure if I ever opened it, it would just say "duct tape and figure it out." The garage was built when I was very young, and I don't remember our home without it except through pictures. I do remember, however, it being new. The whole family wanted to hang out there. It was the spot when it was new before fading into manhood bliss and eventual junk hoarding.

That kerosene heater kept us warm during the ice storm of 1998, in which we lost power for ten days during Christmas break. We weren't too far out in the country. We lived in a large neighborhood that was filled with kids riding bikes, playing baseball, and getting into trouble. Our house was settled at the back of this childhood paradise. When I was little, I remember we had a field of cows behind our house separated by a rickety barbed-wire fence. The cows and field were owned by a friend's father, Torsen Peterson. His daughter, Ginny, went to school with me from kindergarten to twelfth grade. The cows soon moved on, and it became a hay field where my friends and I would play capture the flag along the woods' edge. The woods at the back of the hay field went all the way to the James River. A smell of catfish and bass fishing that I can still remember today.

The smell of the small pond behind our neighbor's house permeated the humid summer air. I caught my first fish on my own there. I was so proud of the happy accident that I ran home with the bass in hand, dripping with pond water and blood to show my dad. He laughed and told me, "That's great! Now go put him back in the water so he doesn't die." I obliged, although I didn't want to quickly send my trophy away in the muddy water. There was a time in my childhood that I would get off the school bus, drop off my backpack in our living room, grab a Little Debbie snack cake and my blue Abu Garcia push-button rod and reel, and head down to the pond to try to recreate that feeling of reeling in a prized fish. Usually, those times either ended in a handful of Brim eating all my worms or just me sitting alone with my thoughts and the sounds of the crickets and cicadas.

I remember the smell of my mom cooking, trying a new recipe that never turned out quite like she had hoped, but she was proud, nevertheless. The rest of us—my dad, sister, and me—rolled our eyes and suffered through whatever the casserole-of-the-week was this time.

As much as she hated it, the best thing my mom would ever cook was the fried chicken thighs she made every Sunday with mashed potatoes, corn, and brown 'n serve rolls. These golden pucks of cast-iron-fried goodness were so prized that friends and neighbors would ask for them during get-togethers, especially during the NASCAR races that came to Richmond twice a year.

The sights, smells, and sounds of those weekends twice a year at the Virginia State Fairgrounds were legendary. It began with my dad taking me to the Busch series race on Friday nights as they were only 250 laps, compared to the 400 laps of the Cup race the next night.

> There's a sense of freedom and innocence that comes with ignorance.

In 1992, my dad decided that it was finally time I graduated to be able to go on Saturdays as well. This is such an iconic moment in my childhood that I still remember how he told me the life-changing news that I would be joining him and his rowdy friends at the track all day to eat junk food, drink my weight in Coke, and squeeze into the sold-out grandstands in turn four, Commonwealth section C. I was standing in our kitchen, its stylings still fresh out of 1982, when my dad entered and handed me a ticket. I was stunned, couldn't believe it was finally happening. It was one of the great moments of my childhood.

To be a kid, growing up through the 1980s and '90s in southern Virginia was magical. We lived about one hundred miles to the ocean, about one hundred miles to the mountains, and on the banks of the James River where America's founders first settled in nearby James-town. We had history and adventure at our fingertips. Looking back, however, I realize the picturesque utopia was anything but.

There's a sense of freedom and innocence that comes with ignorance.

What I didn't know then was that my dad was a compulsive liar, alcoholic, racist, and terrible with money management. Dad had charge cards to Lowe's Home Improvement, Sears, JCPenney, and just about anywhere else that was dumb enough to let him have a big credit line. I remember being taken to JCPenney once a year before the school year began to get us any clothing we needed—all on the charge card, of course. I was too young to notice how unhealthy that was, spending beyond our means.

He and mom not only slept in separate beds but in separate bedrooms, which, until I was a teenager, I thought was completely normal. This explains why their marriage was anything but ideal. They fought constantly. Mom nagged, dad yelled. Although things never got physical, they seemed to hate each other at times—so much so that I remember mom telling my sister and I when we grew up and left the house that she was leaving too. She never did. I never asked why.

Mom had struggles of her own. Though she tried her hardest at encouraging us to be wise with our money, she was always scraping to get by with five dollars in the gas tank, charging our constant grocery needs to the locally owned grocery store where they had our phone number on file for us to use as credit at the store. I often wonder if her love of yard sales was out of the necessity to be thrifty or if she truly enjoyed dressing us in the hand-me-down clothing of strangers. My sister and I hated it then, although later in life we began to enjoy the same hunt our mom did at local yard sales and antique stores. Mom did her best to encourage us to have a relationship with Jesus, although it seemed that her own faith was pretty limited to Sunday mornings with the occasional Saturday morning back-porch Bible reading before returning inside the house for the endless loads of laundry, dirty dishes, and constant cleaning up after all of us. She would drop my sister off at our large church's youth group on Wednesday nights periodically, hoping something would stick, something would get through to her. Later, we would learn that my sister was waiting for mom and me to drive away from the drop-off line before she snuck off with a few friends to galivant around town hanging out with God knows who doing God knows what.

My sister would become the bane of my mother's existence. Not as much my dad, because for him, it seemed he was more comfortable (something that was of highest priority to him) ignoring the troubles of his family. He left that to my mom. Occasionally, things would get bad enough for my dad to notice; he would snap into anger, yelling and spanking when we were young. We grew up fearing him, but not in the "fear God" kind of way. There wasn't respect attached to it. There was only fear.

As the years pressed past childhood innocence and into teenage angst for my sister, the intensity only picked up in our home. She would get into some kind of trouble, there would be yelling, stomping, slamming doors, all while I would be crying, wishing it would stop.

This is what I mean when I refer to being ignorant of my surroundings. In a sense, I thought everything in our family was completely normal and just wanted things to go back to the utopia I thought we lived in. I hated having to tiptoe around dad, listening to mom's constant complaining, and praying my sister would just behave and get herself straight. I wished we could always live in the Myrtle Beach daze type of lifestyle I loved so much when we vacationed there twice a year (which we couldn't afford).

What I didn't know then was how completely dysfunctional we

really were. Ironically, I would later learn just how completely normal all of that dysfunction was. I would catch little glimpses of my neighborhood friends' and cousins' interactions with their families and would sense something was amiss there too. I brushed this off and didn't think too much about it because it felt safer if I didn't dwell on it.

I was a sensitive kid. I remember my dad and sister teasing me on vacations because I was scared to jump into the deep end of a hotel pool. I would get upset, run to my mom for comfort, and she would console me while growing all the more bitter toward my dad. I cried a lot as a child, but in fairness, it didn't take much for me to cry. Every family has a sensitive kid. That was me in our family. If things didn't go my way, if I got a cross look from anyone, if I didn't like what mom cooked for dinner, I would cry.

I vividly remember one incident where this sensitivity helped me escape possible jail time. When I was about ten years old, running around the neighborhood with my friends and vigilantes of the same age, we would get into all sorts of mischief. A little mischief never hurts anyone, but like most things, it can get out of hand quickly. After school one day, we all ventured back in the woods to explore and play. We went deeper into the forest than we ever had before and stumbled upon a shack full of tools and outdoor equipment. Some of my friends thought it would be fun to go inside and explore it while others thought it best to stand outside and throw rocks at the windows for fun. Since I legitimately feared my dad and did not want to cause my family any more drama than what my sister, now sixteen years old, was beginning to cause, I got the hell out of there and went home. The next night, a police officer showed up wanting to talk with me about the shack in the woods. Since I didn't do anything wrong, I stated my innocence and told them exactly what happened. My dad came to my defense.

"Officer, he has to be telling the truth, otherwise he'd be crying by now." And that's how my sensitivity kept me out of what I was sure would have been juvenile detention.

As you can probably conclude by now, the "normalcy" of my childhood could easily lead to mental health struggles down the road as an adult if unresolved. While most of you probably shared similar experiences as a child, you may not have been able to connect the dots yet on how damaging those years may have been.

Now, as a parent, I have gone to some extreme, and often unhealthy, measures to assure that my kids don't have a similar childhood that leads to adult struggles. No matter my story, their story, or your story, ignored drama or tension will always lead down a path of mental and emotional struggle. I've learned how to not protect my kids from drama, but rather to be open about it. Apologize when I need to. Own up to my mistakes and have an open dialogue about what is going on in their lives. My parents never had conversations with us. For them, no news was good news. They would blindly move forward as if everything was completely fine until it wasn't. Then, instead of conversation, it was confrontation. This in part led Sarah, my wife, and I to both commit to having a house that talks about what's going on and resist the urge to yell.

Yelling is a trigger for the both of us. Even if it's just hollering to scrounge up the kids at dinner, we have committed to not doing it. We aren't perfect here, but when we catch ourselves slipping into this "loud talking," we are quickly reminded that it's not the atmosphere we want to raise our children in.

If only my parents had instilled such a simple boundary, how different my childhood may have been. In their defense, neither of them had much to look up to as examples of how to love and nurture a family.

Both of my parents came from broken homes. My dad's father left when he was only six years old. As the oldest boy, he was left to be the father figure to his four brothers and sisters. Talk about growing up quickly! My mom's mother was the spitting image of my sister, both in looks and behavior. She drove away her husband with her immaturity when my mom was just a baby in Norfolk, Virginia.

My sister never took to faith, possibly because what she saw represented in my mother wasn't any sort of heavenly peace we sang about in church. But I decided I couldn't face life alone without a savior, and I gave my life to the Lord at age eleven. My dad came to watch me be baptized then volunteered to take me home to rid me of my wet clothes while the Wednesday night service continued in his rearview mirror.

Despite our childhoods, none of us are perfect. None of our childhoods are perfect. It's cliche to think that all of our problems stem from our upbringing, but sadly, often it's true. While in our most formative years, drama or trauma is magnified in our subconscious, hidden away until we replay them as adults. I was growing up and retreating inwardly all at the same time.

CHAPTER TWO

THE MUSIC IN ME

<hr>

I grew up in a musical home. Not in the traditional sense where mom and dad were both musicians and siblings older than me played multiple instruments. My mother dabbled at piano, and she bought a maple-colored upright that sat in our living room for as long as I can remember. Now, for clarity purposes, our *living room* was different from our *den*. In our tri-level home, the living room sat on the middle level next to the kitchen. Most families would have called it a dining room, but for some reason, we didn't. It was the room full of mom's china, cherished old photos, and a couch that we were not allowed to sit on unless we had company. At times, it felt like an awkward waiting room at a funeral home. There could be some irony there, who knows.

My sister took piano lessons for years in my early life, and we attended her annual recitals while she awkwardly, and sometimes painfully, got through her performance. She and mom would often argue about her practicing, so that was fun.

My dad was the most musical of all of us at the time. He loved music so much, I seldom remember a time when he didn't have it playing around him. Oldies were the anthems of his youth, mixed in with some occasional classic and southern rock. If he was feeling saucy, we listened to the local country station K95 pretty regularly. My childhood was full of cassette tapes. Mostly blank cassette tapes that dad would record his favorite old songs on from the radio whenever they came on. This was playlist-making before it was cool. My dad had quite the collection of mix-tapes and store-bought albums.

One of my most vivid recurring childhood memories is my dad calling me downstairs in the middle of one of his listening parties, in which he sat grinning on the edge of the couch with our home stereo system blasted way up with a cold Natural Light next to him, toes tapping along to whatever song he was infatuated with that week. He would tell me to sit down and listen to this one unique part of a song that he found fascinating. He would rewind it multiple times to make sure I heard what he heard. He was on cloud nine, and I didn't know then that my brain was being trained for a musical ear I would soon put to good use.

When I was twelve years old, I learned of my dad's musical past. He started playing drums when he was twelve years old in Hopewell, Virginia with the friends of his youth. They modeled themselves after the Motown craze of the early 1960s. Matching suits, combed hair, a full rhythm and horn section included. Back then, local bands were special. Everyone wanted to be in one, but only a handful played the circuit of a growing community full of baby boomers. My dad was in several iterations of the same band back then. By the time he was fifteen years old, his band, Exit 6 (the exit number off the local highway to their town), played the sock hops, school dances, and house parties after Friday night football.

My dad would speak of these glory days with such pride, and he longed to go back and do it all again. Around 1996, my dad was invited to reunite with the remaining living members of the crew of bands that populated his hometown to pay tribute and raise money for a scholarship fund in honor of one of the fallen local heroes of their day, Ted Blanks. They rehearsed for months. My dad dug out his old drum kit from his youth, the same kit featured in so many photos I would soon be privy to. The kit, made in 1963 by a German company named Roxy, was a beautiful blue oyster pearl. Unbeknownst to me, this treasure laid dormant in the crawl space of our home my whole life. My dad resurrected the drums from their cold, damp grave and began to restore them in hopes of being able to play them at this upcoming reunion of sorts.

The kit needed more work than he had time for. The next week, I came home from middle school one day to hear the sound of drums playing from the street. The closer I got to my front door, I could hear a familiar cassette tape being played in tandem with the crisp, live percussion. I entered our den to find my dad smiling and playing drums along with the music like he was in high school again.

This was the moment real music entered our home, and I was hooked. My dad gave me the full tour, explaining every inch of these brand-new, piano-black drums from Pearl with shiny Sabian cymbals and chrome hardware. He explained toms, snares, and how each mechanism worked. Then he handed me the sticks and asked if I wanted to try. I could hardly believe it. That first time was so very clunky, but I remember vividly feeling like it was an extension of my body. The pieces and how they simultaneously all worked together just seemed to make sense to me.

The reunion event came and went, and by that time, I had been playing religiously after school each day in our den. I practiced so much that my dad would have to force me to take a break so he could practice. Dad continued to refurbish his old kit to the best of his abilities, now with a mission of me learning to play on the same kit he learned to play on. We bought some cheap plastic cymbals from the JCPenney catalog and new drumheads from the local music store, Music World. I proudly cleared a space in my tiny bedroom to set them up and bang away on them every waking hour.

Later that year, at Christmas, my dad surprised me with a new kit of my own. A brand-new set of sapphire blue pearl Yamaha Stage Custom drums. I purchased new cymbals, which I bought on a layaway plan from the local music store and learned how much it cost to play music quickly. Like any other passion in life, the expenses are as endless as the possibilities before me when seated on that drum throne. Over the next few months, I added some better cymbals to my freshly minted kit, and I was now feeling like a pro ready to go on tour.

I enrolled in the school band program and said yes to every playing engagement I could. Talent shows, garage bands, and a local playhouse production of the musical Annie (my first real paying gig; I made $75). Before I knew it, I was practicing weekly in a sweaty living room with a few other friends that played instruments too. Together, we formed a band called Xtortion, for no other reason than it sounded badass. We covered a loud and lengthy version of "Free Bird" with my friend, Paul Lee, on keys. That dude would warm up playing Beethoven with his eyes closed. Incredible. Dean Crimes on bass, the insanely talented John Spurling and Jamie Price on guitars, along with the energetic eye candy of a front man, Mike Vedomske. We played every chance we got and even put together tour shirts of all the places we played in 2000.

I was also in pep band (playing at basketball games), jazz band (the only other school ensemble that let you play a drum kit), concert band (the high school orchestra), and marching band. Any chance I had to play or be involved with anything that had the letters M-U-S-I-C in it, I couldn't sign up fast enough. I tore up the tri-city roads practicing, playing, and learning every day.

Discovering myself back then felt so much easier than it seems for my own children. Honestly, it felt easier then than it does now that I'm forty. Maybe it's because as adults, we tend to overcomplicate things. When you're young, you're too naive to have fear. You feel like you're going to live forever, so you might as well start as soon as the world around you says it's permissible.

I never gave much thought to my future other than that I wanted to be a studio musician because I once heard how much money they make without having to leave their families alone for months at a time while touring. I was free, and I intended to live my life free of the drama that was rising to new levels at home.

My dad may have created a monster when he brought home a new drum kit back in 1996. I was gone so much playing music that it soon strained our relationship a bit, but honestly no different than any other father and son would have. I certainly didn't think too much of it other than that he might just be jealous that I'm living in the glory days he wished he still had. He would often tell me to enjoy it, make the most of it, that high school was the best years of his life, but then he'd be mad that I was never home anymore. This perplexed me. He was the one that lit this fire in me, and now he was angry because I was going and doing what we both loved? I shrugged it off and didn't give it much real estate in my mind then, but that poke never left me. For me, I wasn't around for a good reason.

My sister was at new levels of rebellion, becoming pregnant when she was nineteen, and I was just thirteen years old. My parents were so disappointed, almost to the point of being left without words. They seemed speechless but determined to love their daughter and this baby no matter what. This "trauma" at home only intensified the fighting, and thus fueled my desire to be away from there, doing what brought me infinite joy. Kaitlyn, my first niece, was born on April 21, 1997. Despite the drama of it all, she became the joy of our home. My dad was instantly smitten, almost to the point where he couldn't help it. Kaitlyn's father, Mike, was very much in the picture. I don't recall exactly when they got a place of their own, but I do remember it being while Kaitlyn was still very young. Before Kaitlyn was born, my mom convinced my sister and Mike to become married in a small, family-only service at our home church at the time. Everyone knew this was less than ideal, just making the best of a less-than-great situation.

I continued to pursue music heavily, and when our garage band eventually fizzled out, I was recruited through a family friend to join an up-and-coming Contemporary Christian Music (CCM) band, covering the likes of Third Day and Jars of Clay, with some originals in the mix. The band mom, also mom to the lead singer and guitar player, was highly motivated and organized all practices and performances. It was my first taste of being in a real band with real shows. We even played a CCM talent show on the TBN network in Charlotte, North Carolina.

That gig transitioned me through the end of high school and into my first year of college in which I attended a local community college while saving the big-money schooling for courses surrounding my eventual major, which was also yet to be determined.

My senior year of high school was so much fun. The senioritis was real, and the teachers embraced it, almost celebratory for us and our soon exit into real life. I continued my stint through all the school bands while playing for the CCM band on the weekends. The highlight of my senior year was graduation. My best friend, Ross, had graduated the year prior, and we were set with some money gifted to me by my dad to head down to Myrtle Beach for "beach week" the day after graduation. My mom threw me a graduation party, and it was the first time I felt like my effort (from kindergarten to twelfth grade) was a celebrated success. I had close friends, band mates, even teachers attend my graduation party. My music teacher, Mr. Warnock, gifted me the latest Rush album on CD. I thought that was the coolest.

The most iconic moment of the week was after the graduation ceremony was over. My dad leaned in to hug me during the procession out of the football field where we celebrated and got our diplomas. Dad leaned in to hug me and said words to me that I didn't know how badly I wanted to hear from him. Words that instantly became iconic in my mind as a moment I would never forget. He stuck his mouth by my ear and whispered through a cracking voice, "I'm proud of you, son." I was in such shock, all I could do was smile and say thank you. It was the first of what would be many times that I would finally hear some vulnerability in my dad's voice while he told me how he really felt. I knew right then and there that my dad's and my relationship would be just fine.

Dad introduced me to music then, and that one simple phrase in that gravel parking lot in Prince George, Virginia, propelled me into the adventure of a lifetime. Things would never be the same. My childhood was officially over. The journey, however, was just beginning.

CHAPTER THREE

TRANSFORMATIVE YEARS

After high school graduation, I set my sights on community college for basic level courses because I was certain that I would have to pay for all of my college. My parents, despite my mother's preaching to us kids on the subject, were never much of savers. By this time, I knew I wanted to pursue music as a full-time career but wasn't sure how. There was no guidebook on how to get started in the music industry. The internet was still a new thing, so I couldn't easily watch YouTube videos to educate myself. All I knew were the stories I had seen on VH1's *Behind the Music*, a TV show I watched religiously before binging shows was even a thing. The artists depicted on that show usually graduated high school or dropped out, packed their bags, and left town for a major city like Nashville, New York City, or Los Angeles to pursue their dreams with little more than the clothes on their back and hopes of making it.

I knew I wanted to make it but was extremely blurry on and unconfident in what that even meant, much less how to obtain it. I assumed college was the smart choice. I was much too afraid to chase my dreams the way they did in the movies or on VH1.

To back up a little bit, early in my senior year, I was informed that one of the best music departments on the east coast was down in North Carolina at East Carolina University. I had never heard of the Pirates, but they came highly recommended by band directors and the like. I went to the campus for a tour with my mom and dad and had scheduled to meet with the dean of percussion in the music department.

I was overwhelmed. This was the biggest campus of anything I had ever seen before. Walking around campus both excited and intimidated me. Kind of that whole "little fish in a big pond" feeling. The campus seemed nice enough, although I distinctly remember the stench of hangover in every corner of that community.

We got to the meeting with the dean, made our pleasantries, thanked him for taking time, and then he dove right in with some questions. Not really an interview, as I was there just to see if this was a place I wanted to even apply to attend. He was, as I soon found out, helping me make one of the biggest decisions of my young life. He asked me about my skills, ambitions, practice routines, etc. Then he asked me a question that I didn't really expect.

"Why do you want to get a degree in music performance?" he asked.

"I want to play music for a living, move to Nashville and become a professional studio drummer," I said proudly.

He replied with an observation, pointing to the wall behind his big university desk. "Do you see those degrees on my wall?"

"Yes," I said.

"Those are three different degrees in music performance from three prestigious music schools," he touted.

Wow, I thought, *this guy must be smart.*

He then said, "I could take all three of those and a dollar and it still wouldn't buy me a cup of coffee." I was confused, laughing nervously because I thought it was a joke, and I wasn't quite sure what he was trying to say. He could see that I was lost, so he put it simply, "If you can play, you don't need a degree to tell others that you can play. Just go do it. There's not a venue, group, or band in the world that would care if you had a music performance degree." Looking at my parents, he continued, "If you want to guarantee income in the music business, the only way is to teach it."

I was deflated. My parents were surprised, but I could easily tell they were relieved. *Well, is this not what am I supposed to do?* I thought. I didn't want to teach some third grader how to play the flute! I hated the flute! I had given the occasional drum lesson, even starting my own business of drum lessons in high school, but I certainly didn't want to spend the rest of my life devoted to that work.

I walked out of the dean's office all the wiser but equally lost on what I was supposed to do next. I was pretty quiet on the drive home up I-95 North, staring out at the endless rows of pine trees, wondering what my purpose was in life. Looking back now, it never dawned on me to just pack my bags after graduation, move to Nashville, and go for it. That was probably from a combination of never having a real-life example in my family or friends of anyone ever chasing a dream to that level and deeply desiring to attend college and start a family afterwards. My sister had started community college but never finished. My father went for one semester at Radford University after he graduated two years late in 1970, but he got in a fight, broke his jaw, came limping back home, and joined the National Guard. My mother moved away from Ohio, where she was raised, the second she graduated high school and went right to work while keeping a keen eye out for a husband that wouldn't disappoint her the way her parents had disappointed her.

I was going to be the first in my immediate family to do this whole college thing, and I knew I could do it. Even though I wasn't the best student, the idea of college never seemed daunting to me; it always excited me. It was an unknown adventure, a chapter I couldn't wait to read.

During senior year of high school, while playing with the contemporary Christian band, I fell in love with worship music. The big anthem-type, stadium rock that centered its affection on the one true God. I felt so connected to God in worship when I was playing music of any kind, but especially when playing worship music in concert or church service settings. While playing with the student group band in my Baptist church, my leaders and youth pastor all suggested I go to this thing called "College for a Weekend" at Liberty University to see if that would be a place for me to attend my post–high school years. As lost as I was after that meeting at East Carolina, I eagerly agreed, hoping to find redemption in some sort of calling with music. By this point, I had accepted that I was going to have to at least start my college career as a music education major, while praying that God would intervene with something else that I was more enthused about.

The weekend came and off I went in a fifteen-passenger van with my fellow seniors in the youth group and the lead singer of the CCM band, my girlfriend at the time. From the moment I pulled onto campus, I knew this was the place for me. Tucked in the foothills of the Blue Ridge Mountains, something about it gave me a sense of possibility and potential that I had never felt before. While Lynchburg was still big I didn't feel lost, I felt at home. The weekend was filled with the complete college experience. We stayed in dorm rooms with real college students hosting us. We ate the food in the dining hall that I would eventually realize was the best during these weekend visits from new prospects. We went to classes that interested us in our respective majors. We went to chapel service, which they called Convocation. They have this convocation service every Monday, Wednesday, and Friday morning at 10:00 a.m. Attendance was mandatory for all undergraduate students, but I didn't care, I loved it. You got to be led by a world-class, student-led worship band playing in a ten-thousand-seat arena with some of the greatest names in evangelical speaking, politics, and business coming to speak to us. What could be better than that?

While there, I discovered there were opportunities to play music on several student-led ministry teams, most that travel, and one that stays on campus and leads all student convocation and church services. Of course I signed up immediately to audition, because, well, music! I remember the audition going well, and my then-girlfriend also auditioned. I left the audition thinking little of it other than that one day I'd really love to play drums for the Campus Praise Band, the one that led music in that convocation service I attended. I could see myself up there, but knew it was a big dream that may not happen.

I left that weekend with an application to attend in my hand, and I couldn't fill it out quick enough. My parents were pleased as Lynchburg was only a short two-hour drive westward down Highway 460, the same highway that ran through our county of Prince George. They were excited to see that I found a place that felt like home and were probably a bit relieved that I would attend a Christian school rather than one that was notoriously known for all-night benders and good ol' fashioned hell-raising.

I mailed in my application because those were the days before email was used for everything. I waited patiently for a reply, and the day the acceptance letter came, it felt like finding a golden ticket to Willy Wonka's chocolate factory. I remember my parents being excited for me, but my dad being a bit shy with his support. I thought nothing much of it but would soon realize just how big of a deal this was to him, personally.

I finished my first year of community college, enrolled, and transferred my credits to Liberty University beginning the fall of 2003. I would enter as a declared music education major but quickly learned what all that meant. It meant mandatory involvement in the marching band, which I entered into with a bit of excitement. This was an opportunity to play, and I accepted that for what it was. But the deeper I got into this major, the more I hated it. The snobbery of the music department and the expectation that my life would be spent in a practice room or fail was not one that excited me for a collegiate experience or career.

I was thrilled to get a call from a ministry team band at Liberty asking me to join their team. This would be a nice little scholarship and a chance to tour on the weekends and take my music career to the next level. I nervously declined the offer. I don't know what I was thinking other than I already have a band that I'm committed to back home, and even though I graduated high school in the top half of my class, I was not a great student. The thought of being away from campus most weekends made me nervous that I would quickly flunk out of college, which was not an option for me. The ministry team was disappointed at my decline to join them, but most importantly, they respected the maturity of my decision of why I declined.

I thought I blew my opportunity but prayed I didn't.

Things in the CCM band were getting increasingly difficult too. Traveling back home for rehearsals and trying to arrange gigs around my new college activities combined with my girlfriend and me going through an eventual breakup all added up to a quick mental breakdown, the first I would ever experience in life.

The breakup was super emotional as I was convinced that we would get married after college. She had other plans of marriage with another guy she'd met in our first semester at Liberty together. I was heartbroken and stuck in a major that I hated with no real friendships yet, as this was all still in my first semester there.

It was suggested by one of our dorm hall RAs that I see a campus counselor. I thought counseling was for crazy people, but I was at the end of my rope and was willing to try anything. I made an appointment and sat down with a Christian counselor who genuinely seemed to care about the students he was guiding. I confided everything in him, and he assured me that what I was feeling was completely normal at my age and stage of life. The idea of being lost when there was really no reason to be may have seemed absurd but was generally normal. That session gave me great relief, and I continued to meet with him for the rest of that semester.

I learned a very important lesson through that counseling and through the quick reveal of God's plan all along. I can trust Him even when I can't see the reasons for my current suffering. That suffering, and my confusion, was short-lived as God was about to change my life forever in a moment that I thought was completely hopeless.

Every December, before break, the dorms would host open houses to show off holiday decorations. It was a big deal because dorms were segregated, male and female, and the sight of a girl on our dorm floor was like being in a teen movie or something. We all took good showers, something rarely done by college boys, and dressed to impress. Going through the dorms that night were the guys that I had auditioned for back at "College for a Weekend" to join a ministry team. Dave McKinney and Adam Lancaster led the Campus Praise Band, the one that I really wanted to be in one day but had given up hope of joining since I turned down the offer from one of the traveling teams. Dave and Adam strolled through my hall that night and waved cordially to me, as they remembered me from my audition. They were like celebrities. "Those are the guys from the band!" people whispered as they walked by.

After they passed my room and waved, Adam quickly turned back around and asked me to stop by his office tomorrow. I eagerly yet suavely replied, "Sure thing." No big deal, just the head of the coolest band on campus asking me to swing by his office, happens all the time.

The next day, I rushed to Adam's office where he informed me that their drummer was graduating midyear after this semester and wanted to know if I would be interested in re-auditioning for their band to take his spot when he left. I couldn't believe it. They sought *ME* out. They wanted *ME* to audition.

This boost of confidence couldn't have come at a better time. Even though things were progressing in counseling, I secretly considered leaving Liberty until I figured my life out. I didn't want to, but I didn't know what else to do.

> I can trust Him even when I can't see the reasons for my current suffering.

The day of the audition came and they threw some of their most difficult songs at me. I had seen the talent on campus, so couldn't believe I was even being considered. I didn't know it at the time, but the position came down to me and one other guy. Had I known I was up against competition, I may have flubbed the audition big time. Instead, it went extremely well. They shook my hands, thanked me for coming in, and told me they would be in touch over the Christmas break with a decision.

I remember being out shopping late one afternoon with my mom and dad back home during the break when my flip phone rang with a number I didn't recognize, but I knew the area code. Lynchburg, Virginia. I nervously answered, and it was Adam, calling to invite me to join their team starting next semester. I couldn't say yes fast enough. He informed me that the position came with a full tuition scholarship.

The only thing I would have to cover was my stay on campus, food, and books. We briefly went over some formalities about returning to campus early to bring me up to speed with the team through a week of rehearsals. I hung up with Adam, my parents looking at me with great anticipation, and mumbled out through a huge smile that I got the position!

It was a level of validation that I never had in my life. I knew I could play, but I didn't know I was good enough to join a team as prestigious as this. My dad proudly proclaimed that he was prepared for either answer, but if it was good news, we would go out to dinner to celebrate. Truth be told, my dad would use any excuse to go out for dinner, but I was on cloud nine and took the reward with glee.

I would finish out my collegiate career playing with that team and forming friendships I still hold dearly today. I got to travel the country to new places during breaks with CCM artist in residence at Liberty at the time, Charles Billingsley. I was able to record live albums and play in front of thousands of people each week, all while having my college tuition paid for. The way God pivoted my life in one semester was incredible, and I still can't believe it.

The difference in mindset that counseling awarded me, a miracle of God's provision of direction in my life, and that one chance encounter in my dorm hall with Adam changed my life forever.

Despite our best efforts when we are in our early adulthood, we cannot write our own stories. We can try, but we'll fail. I will say, however, I do believe God has to take us all through events like this early in life to teach us that His plans are far greater than our little minds can scheme up for ourselves.

When I realized for the first time that, in my relationship with God, He would take care of me even when I couldn't take care of myself, the stress from years of growing up with a failure mindset began to chisel away. This first test of provision would certainly not be my last—far from it—and things would get worse for me before they got better, but I was able to hold my head high with the confidence that if God was for me, even I couldn't be against me.

That's a powerful truth when you realize that the thoughts that seem to dominate your everyday life are not from a God who loves you and wants what's best for you. They're from an enemy that I would get to know more and more as the years went forward. I didn't befriend the enemy, but I became familiar with his tactics that kept me from experiencing freedom from my little human mind and the limitations, lies, and doubts that were often conjured up with his help.

I went on to finish my college career at Liberty in 2006, but more than any degree, I learned a lifetime of lessons in faith, music, and relationships in my short three-year term there. Those years undoubtedly shaped me and prepared me for the road ahead. Not one filled with fame, but ultimately making it to thrive with a beautiful life I couldn't wait to start.

CHAPTER FOUR

I GUESS I'M AN ADULT NOW?

Over my break from college in the winter of 2004, I began to pursue a relationship with Sarah, a girl I had grown up with, yet we were on opposite sides of the county. Her brother and I were good friends, but Sarah and I never really knew each other until high school, especially once she began attending the same church I did. We found ourselves in similar circles in high school, and even though I was dating someone else at the time, she asked me to prom her senior year. I chose to decline (I know, I know) because I was dating another girl, but it set a tone in my mind of, *Wow, she must like me. I didn't see that coming.* She was fun, energetic, attractive, and had a wonderful family.

During that winter break, we went out as friends with a group of people, and I soon realized she could be *the one.*

Sarah was attending an internship program for post–high school graduates in Garden Valley, Texas at the time, and part of this ministry was a commitment to not date for your first year there. A commitment I soon became aware of as I felt myself falling in love with her over our many phone calls, exceeding call limits on our parents' cell phone plans. She would be eligible to date on March 1, 2005, after completing half of a second year as a leader on campus.

We talked almost every day while I was finishing up my junior year at Liberty and she was in another time zone in east Texas. She had sent me a mysterious letter to hold onto without opening until March first and had written on the back "be anxious in nothing," quoting scripture from the book of Philippians. That was pure torture, and I had to give the letter to my college roommate to keep me from opening it before that fateful day. I had hoped that in it, she would tell me how she felt about me, and we would spend our lives together. All of that came true when I stayed up until 1:00 a.m. (12:00 a.m. Texas time) as the calendar changed into March. I called her, and she asked me to open the letter while she read it aloud to me with a copy she had made for herself before mailing it to me. She explained how the past few months of getting to know me had been and, to my surprise, she went on to explain how she had feelings for me dating back to when we were mere acquaintances in high school. I had no idea; I felt so foolish, but equally flattered.

We began a long-distance dating relationship that night that quickly whisked me away on my first flight ever at twenty-one years old to go visit her in Texas, our first time as a couple. She showed me all around Dallas, where I flew into, and we had our first date, sharing an order of chicken tenders at the top of Reunion Tower.

Although we didn't escape our share of challenges that a young couple in a long-distance relationship faces, we both knew we were in this for the long haul.

That summer, I interned at a church in Orlando, Florida and we began planning a self-guided Christian mission trip to Rome, Italy. Both of us being artists, we felt called to minister to other artists, and Italy is full of them. We planned to go live amongst them for a week, get to know them, set up in the park, paint and play music, and share how Jesus had changed our lives. The church I was interning at believed in us so much that they raised money to send us over there. Once the tickets were bought, my plans of proposing quickly shifted from popping the question on her front porch, the same place where we had discussed being married one day, to the obvious: Rome, Italy. I bought the ring before we left on the trip using student loan money and held onto it as if my life depended on it. I traveled the two hours back to our hometown and took her family out to dinner at their favorite restaurant in Richmond to ask for their blessing to ask Sarah to marry me. They were ecstatic and lovely. At that dinner, I asked her brother to be my best man. Everything was perfect, and I was set to pop the question in Italy in November 2005.

The trip came, and we barely had time to land and drop off our bags at the hostel before the ring was burning a hole in my pocket. We went into immediate tourist mode and went straight to the Vatican City. We walked into Saint Peter's Square, surrounded by beautiful, ancient architecture and fountains. *This is the place*, I thought. I got down on one knee, an family of tourists nearby started freaking out and taking pictures, and I asked her to be my wife. Somewhere, a family on the other side of the world has pictures of this moment. From there, we toured the area, had the best pasta of our lives and got on with the reason we went on the trip to begin with.

We got back home, I finished up at Liberty, and the wedding was set for June 24, 2006. We were married in the midsummer heat and humidity of southeast Virginia on the front porch of her parents' home, her childhood home. It was so special. Our life together was just beginning.

After a honeymoon in the Outer Banks of North Carolina, we packed up a U-Haul full of my things and moved me into her studio apartment in downtown Chicago. Our first year of marriage would be in a six-hundred-square-foot home in which the kitchen was also the bedroom, the dining room, and the living room. Near the corner of LaSalle and Division, we set out on our own to figure out what being together looked like for the first time in our relationship. We had bills; not many, but they were there. We had no vehicle—we only needed a monthly public transportation pass to get around. Sarah worked at Starbucks in the mornings and attended art school in the afternoons and evenings. I applied for jobs and ended up being hired at Career-Builder. I had no idea what I was doing; I just knew I was an adult now, or so I was told, and I needed to get a job. We knew that we were only in Chicago while Sarah finished school, so I didn't look for any full-time ministry jobs up there, but I kept ministering at a large church in the suburbs after a friend I played music with at Liberty invited me to come out and play with them on the weekends. So each weekend, we would take public transportation to the Metra station, then take that train out into the suburbs where we would be picked up by someone else on the worship team. We would then be taken to the church for rehearsals and Saturday evening service followed by dinner and a guest bedroom with a band member before getting up Sunday for an early call time back at the church and two more services. Then, we would take the Metra train back into the city and the CTA (Chicago Transit Authority) train back to our little home.

This was how we spent our weekends just about the whole year that we lived in Chicago. I ended up being brought on as an intern at that church, and they gave me some great stage time leading worship for their college ministry. It was such a blessing and much needed real church experience after being in the Liberty bubble for the past few years.

My day job at CareerBuilder was a joke. Apparently, I was supposed to be selling ads for job openings in the Orlando, Florida market from my cubicle in Chicago next to the airport. It's here that I learned quickly that I was no longer in the safe confines of Liberty University because suddenly Christianity was not the accepted norm, rather it was joked about and curse words abounded in weekly meetings. I was so lost there, but it paid the bills—until it didn't. Like I said, I was terrible at this job, and they eventually saw that, and so they decided to let me go. I felt like such a failure riding the CTA train back to our tiny apartment to explain to my new wife that the paychecks wouldn't be coming in much longer. Her amazing parents sustained us during that season the way they have countless times since. Soon, after a few temp jobs, I landed a steady gig until it became clear to both of us that the call to full-time ministry was now, and not whenever Sarah finished school in Chicago.

Being kids of the Southeast, we loved home and knew that was where we wanted to set some roots. Maybe not in Virginia, but nearby, like in one of the Carolinas or Georgia (Florida was not considered the South where we grew up).

It turns out, however, in the wild world of ministry, you cannot simply tell God where you are willing to go and expect Him to comply. I must have sent over a hundred resumes to churches in the Southeast and not one of them even so much as acknowledged that they received desire from me. We eventually understood what God was trying to tell us and submitted to going wherever He wanted us to go. I began applying to churches all over the US: Texas, Washington, Colorado, California, Indiana, and yes, even Florida. Just for laughs, God even gave us a fly-in weekend at a church in West Palm Beach, Florida, but we didn't feel the call there and, soon after the trip, removed our name from consideration.

We then had several interviews with a small Baptist church in Indiana in the suburbs of Indianapolis. I had never been to or seen Indiana in my life, with the exception of driving through with our U-Haul on the move from Virginia to Chicago. I remember thinking, *I wonder where the racetrack is?* and never gave Indiana another thought in my mind.

We took a weekend interview at that church in Greenwood, Indiana, and immediately felt at peace, like we were home. Even though it was a Baptist church—which, after being raised in one, I was not looking to work in—I felt like I could help grow this ministry and build the church up into the modern age.

In the summer of 2007, after a year of marriage, I accepted a worship pastor position there, and we moved from the city of Chicago to the suburbs of Indianapolis, not knowing what all God had in store for us as we continued to rapidly grow from kids to adults.

Nothing prepares you to be thrown into the world of adulthood (moving, bills, responsibilities, insurance) like actually stepping out in faith and moving twelve to fifteen hours from everything and everyone you ever knew. But we were committed. We wanted to plant roots here and naively told the Lord we would stay here for the long haul, even though he had other plans for us stubborn kids.

All while my life was moving in fast forward at the age of twenty-three, I still hadn't dealt with some of the anxiety and anger that reared when I was in college. It was almost like the further I moved away from home, the more my battle with mental health began to surface. This separation from my roots must have made room for the Lord to reveal to me the battle I had always been in. It wasn't even the typical stresses of adulthood that set me off, it was having unrealistic expectations in my mind of the way certain things were supposed to go and how certain people were to behave.

It took a long time—like, an embarrassingly long time—for me to learn that people are never what I wanted them to be: perfect. Maybe because I expected perfection from myself—I don't know—but I was consistently let down by people and surrounding situations, and it was beginning to take a toll on me and my new life.

Expectations of marriage in the early years are easy to live up to for the most part. We had some decent pre-marital counseling that allowed us to set some expectations immediately. Combine that with the rose-colored glasses of being newlyweds, and marriage seemed easy.

The false narratives entered my mind beginning with my career. At Liberty, I was surrounded by top notch, compensated musicians and vocalists. We played together six times a week, and we easily, and quickly, reached that level of nonverbal communication that only musicians can understand. With a simple look or twitch of a leg, we knew what the other was thinking and where they were going musically. Now, I was leading a team of volunteer musicians that had real jobs, and music or worship leading was not their entire life like it had been mine at Liberty. How was I supposed to take a ragtag team and teach the same intuition that I shared with my bandmates at Liberty? This tension grew increasingly frustrating and led to many dumb decisions by me in the early years of ministry. Ministry is supposed to be about people, but to me it had become, and would remain for a while, about the product. This had to be beaten out of me by life, failure, and the Lord, but not before I would allow it to take root in my mind that everyone just disappoints me.

This was the lie that I allowed to take up residence for a long time and would set a trajectory of constant depression, poor attitudes, and my eventual moment of declaration that I couldn't do this anymore.

I know this sounds like things escalated quickly, but understand, this is just a preview into my thoughts as I was setting the groundwork for things to get out of control, and the next several years would be a harvest of all that I allowed to be sowed in my mind.

CHAPTER FIVE

REAL LIFE: STARTING A FAMILY

After being surrounded by young, growing families of our small church in the suburbs of Indianapolis, our initial plan of waiting five years before having our first child quickly gave way to the baby fever Sarah was feeling while constantly attending baby showers and visitations to the local labor and delivery wing of the hospital. In the winter of 2009, we decided to pull the trigger and began trying to have our first child. When trying to make such an emotional addition to your world, patience flies right out the window. We tried for a few months to no avail, which added to the stress hormones in our little apartment home as Sarah became more and more discouraged.

Then one morning as spring was beginning to bloom in early 2010, she woke me, gasping with excitement, with the news that we had a positive pregnancy test. I was equally relieved and immediately frightened, as most fathers-to-be are in this scenario. This was the most real-life event that I can remember in my life to that point. Marriage seemed easy to comprehend as the other person joining in life with you already exists. They had a face, a personality, and experiences that they brought to the table. A newborn child that we would now be responsible for? That brought so much mystery, and with it, the anxiety of the unknown. Would we have enough money? Where would we live?

What would this baby be like? Would we be good parents? Would we make similar mistakes our parents made? If so, would that damage the child?

I instantly began to write the what-if scenarios in my mind and could hardly celebrate the news as unreasonable and unrealistic expectations took on a new topic in my mind: my unborn child. I knew, one hundred percent, that I wanted to have a boy first. We had long since discussed how ideal it would be to have one boy and one girl. That was the family dynamic that we both grew up in and loved it. We felt like one child would be lonely and probably a bit too spoiled, and three kids would divide our attention so much that we couldn't give each of them the time they deserve. Again, we began to write the story ourselves rather than trusting what God wanted (however, spoiler alert, this is also what God had in mind for us—probably because He knew our limitations as much as we anticipated they would be).

> I already started writing the unborn child's story.

In my family, the baby girl came first—my older sister. In Sarah's family, the baby girl also came first—her. So, we thought this may repeat to our family, but, oh, how I prayed against it. I wanted a boy to play with, take to races, drive around late at night, listen to music . . . all the things I loved about my childhood with my dad, I wanted for my own.

Do you see how I already started writing the unborn child's story the same way I tried to write my own story?

Time came for the ultrasound in which we were able to find out the gender of the baby. I went into the room expecting to be disappointed and had mentally prepared myself to love the baby no matter, despite how vocal I was against having a girl first. I knew that I needed to control my reaction if it didn't go my way. Sarah was hormonal enough. The last thing she needed was me being outwardly dejected about the gender of our unborn child.

The ultrasound technician zoomed in, zoomed out, adjusted Sarah's belly and got the baby to turn where she could get a better look. I looked on helplessly, anxiously awaiting the news. She then zoomed back into the baby's genital area on the screen, drew an arrow to a curved section and asked if we knew what we were looking at. I so badly wanted to shout, "Is it a penis?!" But instead I just shook my head, quietly motioning to her that I did not in fact know what I was looking at. The screen looked like some amoeba under a microscope in tenth grade biology class. She announced that it was a penis and that we were having a boy.

Now, to say this was the greatest day of my life may be a bit unfair, especially since I happened to find the one true love of my life, we fell in love, and we were engaged in a fairy-tale way. I had success in college as a musician, having my collegiate studies paid for by talents the Lord had gifted me. I had been raised by two incredible parents who stuck it out through thick and thin and both loved me very much. But this hit differently. I was going to be a boy dad. So many times, as a kid, I would think to myself, and occasionally share with my dad, how I couldn't wait to do some of the things we were doing at that moment with my son one day, and now the day of confirmation was here: I would have a son.

I was over the moon. Nothing else mattered. No amount of disappointment in people could get me down. Our parents were ecstatic and couldn't wait to be grandparents—Sarah's parents for the first time, and my parents for the third time.

Time seemed to drag on for the rest of the pregnancy, as we couldn't wait to meet him. We had previously decided on two girl names and two boy names, each with a priority in case we had one of each. I knew that I wanted my first son to share the same middle name that my Pawpaw (grandfather), dad, and I all bore: Glenwood. My Pawpaw actually went by Glen his whole life because his full name was Overton Glenwood Pead. His parents decided to call him Glen, a popular name at the time. My dad was his first born and carried the middle name: Merle Glenwood Pead. My dad carried it on to me, his first-born, seemingly making it a tradition: Dustin Glenwood Pead. Being as sentimental as I had always been, it was a no-brainer to carry on the name to my firstborn son: Ethan Glenwood Pead. Now, I wish I could tell you that we chose Ethan because of a family heritage, or even after the Ezrahite in the book of Psalms, but no, not that epic. One of our favorite movies of that time were the *Mission Impossible* remakes with Tom Cruise whose character name was Ethan Hunt. We loved that name. It seemed manly, yet approachable. A little bit tough, but mostly regal sounding. So yes, we named our son after a movie character, but not because we were huge Tom Cruise fans, just because we loved the sound of the name.

Ethan Glenwood Pead was born on Monday, October 18, 2010, making Sarah and me first-time parents. I remember being in the delivery room with Sarah's mom, Tracy, as we each held one of Sarah's legs back to help her deliver her first child. Admittedly, I'm a crier. I cry often. And his moment of arrival was no different. I cried looking at him. I cried looking at Sarah. I cried as I muttered over and over again in disbelief, "He's here." At that moment, I got it. I understood what parents had for centuries described as the miracle of childbirth. Don't get me wrong, it's a disgusting process, but the end result is a true miracle: life. And this was a life that I was now responsible for. I remember thinking, at twenty-six years old, "I'm just a kid, how do I

HAVE a kid?!"

This thought was nearly crippling. I felt like I still had so much to learn before being responsible for another human life that cannot take care of themselves. All of the what-if worries I had before his arrival were now a full-force reality in my mind. I didn't want him to grow up in a home of yelling, drama, and crossing of emotional boundary lines like I did. I did, however, want him to grow up with a sense of family, community, and adventure with his father the way I did. But how do I manifest these hopes and dreams? Instead of being motivated, my mind crippled at the cusp of decision and future-shaping. I was frozen in time—in fear—of what might become of Ethan's life, our lives.

All this was churning in my mind while becoming incrementally better at my job. Understanding the real people of suburbia rather than the professionals I was used to was beginning to take place in my heart. I started to understand a clear vision of where I felt like we needed to go. I began building a team to get us there and moved full steam ahead without permission or thought from anyone, including my boss. (Yikes. This would come back to bite me later.)

Since things were going so well at work, where the majority of my identity was found, I ignored and pressed down all the thoughts that were overwhelming at home and found some sense of rest in how amazing a mother Sarah was. She was so good with Ethan. She was the one that got up in the middle of the night most nights, and she sat home alone with him while I was at midweek rehearsal. I found my place at home by making sure all bills were paid on time and cooking dinner every chance I got.

The patience of being a first-time father was rough in the first couple of years. I did not grow up in the most patient of environments, and it's something that still hinders me at times today. Thinking about it now, I think it mostly stems from a sense of discontentment: discontentment with where I lived, financial status, and opportunities I wish I had. You always believe, when you're young, that where you grow up hinders you. It wouldn't be until I moved away for a few years that I realized just how much that place shaped me into who I was, and who I was becoming still. Money was a hot button issue when I was a kid. I thought we spent more at times because we had more to spend, but in reality, it was creating a debt tension in our home that could be felt. I so badly didn't want to take that into my adult family, but this lack of contentment was always there, urging me to spend more to feel more content. I remember feeling like no one from where I grew up ever amounted to much more than a successful local realtor with a country club membership and kids that secretly did drugs and won popularity contests. I never believed anyone could leave for anything better than that. So, in a sense, me leaving felt like I had won, but it made me feel so very lost.

All of these conflicts in my mind went unaddressed through the birth of Ethan and the few years that followed. We knew we wanted to have a second child, prayerfully a girl, and we wanted Ethan to be out of diapers by the time they were born. So, doing the math, we began trying for our second child when Ethan was two years old. This time, it took pretty quickly, and by November of 2012 we were informing our family in person while we hosted Thanksgiving that we were indeed expecting our second child in early July of 2013.

My mindset was, *Well, the first one hasn't killed us, so how hard could a second one be?* I was more excited than nervous this time. Things were still going well at work, and we hadn't made any major mistakes with Ethan at that point, so I welcomed it as we began to pray that this new human growing inside of Sarah was a little baby girl. I wanted it for Sarah more than anything. I had my boy, my friend, my pal to go camping, attend races, and see baseball games with. I wanted her to have the little girl that she dreamed of as a child to dress up, brush hair, and co-host tea parties. The two-kids-and-a-little-white-house American dream was shaping up perfectly for us. We had very little debt, despite my efforts to negate that. We had great friends, excellent neighbors, and a church that we were plugged into. On the outside, life was perfect.

However, on the inside, I could feel an even bigger sense of anxiety welling up in me. I had always been an emotional person. Even as a kid, it didn't take much to make me cry. And as any parent could attest, having kids of your own makes you even more of a sap: crying at commercials, the sound of their laughs, and so on. So, needless to say, being this emotional at my core, it was much easier for depression to take root.

My parents were aging rapidly as, shortly before Ethan was born, my dad was forced into early retirement by a pair of bum knees that he abused for years at the paper mill. This sudden change in life manifested itself into full-blown alcoholism. He had always been a drinker. Beer every day and bourbon on his days off and vacations. But I never witnessed it get out of hand outside of regular angry hangovers that were taken out on my sister, mom, and me. His identity as the breadwinner was stripped from him, a title he had held since he was eleven when his dad left his family. He had no sense of purpose, it seemed. Thus, the drinking got out of control. He combined hard liquor with sleeping pills as if to disappear in slumber from the crisis he now faced. Because he was never much of a saver or financial planner, they had very little to live on.

This obviously put a new level of stress on my parents' marriage.

As my life was all coming together "perfectly," everything they knew was falling apart. My sister was now on her way to being incarcerated by her decision to forge signatures on blank checks from anyone she could steal them from, including my parents and grandmother. She had two kids from two different men and was completely lost in life. All of this took place in south central Virginia while I was building my utopia seven hundred miles away in central Indiana with my new, growing family.

My mother had always struggled with boundaries with me. As mentioned in earlier chapters, she would often confide in me how much she hated and resented my dad and how she wished he would "get his act together." When I was young, I would watch sitcoms with my parents like *Home Improvement* or *Roseanne* and figured it was completely normal and acceptable for this type of undermining and inappropriate commentary. America seemed to laugh at it. It was reality for us, and I just accepted it for what it was at the time. I watch reruns of these shows now in shock of what we found acceptable.

But as I grew older, their troubles increased along with my emotional distance. That didn't stop my mom from continuing to reach out about all of her complaints in life. I seldom received a phone call from her that wasn't a complaint of some sort, or news of what trouble my dad and sister were in now. My fuse became shorter and shorter with each phone call and awkward visit. It got to the point where I would much rather stay with Sarah's family when we traveled home because my childhood home was such a mess, so dysfunctional. I wanted so badly to show my son where I learned to ride my bike, my childhood bedroom, and the great neighborhood I grew up in. But just like everything else in life, that shine had quickly faded by this time. I wanted to be proud to show Ethan where I was from; instead, I was embarrassed.

Sarah's family and their home was a place of rest, for the most part. Her parents knew we were more comfortable there and quietly, and happily, accommodated us with each visit home, even though we tried to be fair with sharing time with each family at their own abodes.

Any newlywed couple with children knows this tension. You want to make everyone happy, and you have so many expectations, as I briefly described, wanting to be proud of where you grew up. This tension eventually became too much to bear and we made the hard, adult decision to stay at her parents' house each time we came home. We would still go visit my family at their home but refused to stay overnight there. As much as it was stressful, it was also so emotionally damaging to me. To drive seven hundred miles with my growing, beautiful family just to be held at arm's length from connecting too deeply due to my parent's lifestyle and home environment. Still, we found time for some precious moments with Ethan and both sets of grandparents.

> Family life was in full swing, but unfortunately, my mental spiral was just beginning to pick up speed.

In the summer of 2013, we were pleasantly surprised that our little nugget, a girl who we would name Aubrey Anne Pead, would not be born in early July, but on our wedding anniversary of June 24th. We had the sweetest experience celebrating our "best anniversary gift ever" in the hospital, the arrival of Aubrey. Our nurse grabbed a white onesie from the nursery and wrote those words across it as a gift to us. It meant so much to us, we framed it and still have it today.

Aubrey was everything opposite of Ethan. Aubrey was a tiny baby; Ethan was a big one. Ethan was quiet and easy to handle. Aubrey was fiery and a handful. Ethan could entertain himself. Aubrey needed constant attention. Ethan was my buddy from the very beginning, but Aubrey had my heart. I've never known the kind of love that a daughter gives unconditionally to a father except through Aubrey. She loves me fiercely. It sustains me in my toughest days when she seems to know just when I need a smile, a hug, a nose kiss.

Family life was in full swing, but unfortunately, my mental spiral was just beginning to pick up speed.

CHAPTER SIX

OVERWHELMED

I remember sitting on the edge of our bed in our small bedroom in Franklin, Indiana with a sense that I couldn't take much more of the anger, frustration, and anxiety that built up in my mind. I was crying and could only think of all that was wrong in my life. The glass for me was never half full, it was always half empty with a drain hole in the bottom of it. My anger and bitterness had gotten such a hold on me that I would scream as loud as I could when alone in my truck to get some sort of release. What you and I probably both know now is that small exercise didn't provide much relief at all; in fact, it fed these out-of-control emotions.

A few months before this crying session, I began to read a book by a pastor named Perry Noble. Perry, though he had his own struggles not listed in this book and that would come to light eventually, shared a raw and honest account of what being in ministry was like while living with depression and anxiety. You see, despite the jokes we made in college, ministry was about and for people. It is the ultimate people business, and I had no idea how to deal with all of their expectations of me on top of my own unhealthy expectations of myself and others. What Perry ultimately shared and that I felt such shame about was that it was okay for a Christian to take medication for depression and anxiety. For so long, I believed that my depression could be prayed away. I prayed, hard and often. I asked for prayer constantly. I had people pray over me, anoint me with oils, and pray in tongues over me. Nothing seemed to work. I was told it was because I didn't have enough faith. Maybe that was true. It did seem too big for me to ever believe it could leave. But in Perry's book, he went on to explain that through his own journey, he realized that some things are just physically jacked up and we need help, people, and medicine to counteract them for a season if necessary, and that was ok.

Back to the moment of me crying at the foot of my bed: Sarah was beside me, exasperated with another uncontrollable overflow of my emotions, something we had both gotten used to over the years with me. Knowing a possible solution, I was looking for any excuse to say yes to seeing a doctor; I just needed a little push. I asked her if she wanted me to see a doctor about it. I didn't ask her if she thought that maybe I should kind of sort of see someone about all of this. She barely hesitated before quietly, but strongly, answering, "Yes."

That was when I knew for sure that this was no longer just affecting me or people that I didn't mind it affecting; it was affecting those that I cared for and loved in my own home. Even to this today, those first few years of my daughter's life I only vaguely recall because I was stuck in my own cycle of negative thinking. I mourn this loss of memory, but her love for me through the years has been more than any reassurance needed for me to know that I am forgiven and loved.

I immediately stood from the bed and made a call to our local physician to schedule an appointment. When asked the reason for my visit over the phone, I still had tears running down my face and adrenaline running through my body as I heard myself utter the words, "Depression and anxiety." The doctor's office receptionist didn't skip a beat, as I'm sure by this point, she had gotten all too used to hearing men and women of my generation calling for the same reasons. Even that thought had me thinking I must not be alone, but also how sad it is that this sort of thing is so rampant. Fast forward to the earliest they could see me, aka a few months later, I was still more motivated than ever to get a cure for this. In the meantime, convinced that I needed more than just medical help with my thoughts and emotions, I reached out to a local biblical counseling service. They got me in immediately, and I was relieved, and a bit excited, for the opportunity to talk with someone about my thoughts that had no skin in the game, no harm from the shrapnel in my harshness that may come out in these sessions. Since I was in the ministry full time, the counseling service was also very affordable. It seemed that everything was lining up for me to "get fixed."

I sat in Brad's office waiting for him to come so we could begin whatever these sessions were going to look like. I was nervous but eager to share—even more eager to fix the problem. Man to man, he explained to me very calmly that there wasn't just a simple fix for what I was experiencing. I had spent over twenty years practicing these thoughts, and they weren't going to go away in just a few sessions. By this point, wounded from having so many Christians instruct me to just have more faith, I made it a point to be clear with Brad when he asked me how much I wanted the Bible to have a part in our sessions. I was honest with him when I said I didn't want to neglect the Truth of God in my life, but I also absolutely didn't want advice to pray harder or to have more faith, because I had already tried that. He laughed and assured me those instructions come from a naive state of mind about mental health, and that quickly put me at ease with him and our future sessions.

For the first few sessions, I unloaded on him my life story, pretty much everything you have read up to this point. I expected Brad's response to be one of shock and utter distaste, but he sat quietly listening, only interjecting with a few questions of clarity and of course the cliche, "How did that make you feel?" He also would often interject to begin rerouting my thought patterns, always with a sarcastic grin that playfully irked my nerves because I knew he was right. Eventually, after a few sessions of hearing my story and giving me enough hope to calm me down and see this process through, we got into the beginning stages of what is known as CBT, or cognitive behavioral therapy. You see, what I had practiced and become a master at over the short couple of decades of my life at that point was to have negative thoughts constantly, letting those thoughts fester and spiral into unfiltered words or behavior that wasn't really who I was deep down. This is why I have always been quick to apologize. Even those that I have hurt the most in my life will tell you to this day how quick I am to apologize for my words or behavior. I learned early on that it seemed out of my control and I didn't really *WANT* to behave that way. This caused me to get sent to principal's offices, suspended from school, asked not to return to teams or clubs, and would eventually lead to a few job changes. I didn't want to be that way. I hated myself for it, which just fed even more into the negative thought spirals and, thus, more poor choices of words and actions.

> I had become a master at having negative thoughts constantly, letting those thoughts fester and spiral into unfiltered words or behavior that wasn't really who I was deep down.

We never got too far into CBT because I would always show up to each session with a new, world-ending thought or perceived problem. But what I did learn through our referencing back often to the basics of CBT is that our thoughts control our emotions which control our behaviors, a lesson I still remind myself and loved ones of continuously today. This was, sadly, eye-opening for me. I knew my thoughts had taken control of my life, but I had never noticed this pattern before. Through these sessions with Brad, I began to clear out the junk of thoughts that I had trained myself to believe and learned to reprogram those thoughts, or the neural pathways, to things that were, as Jon Acuff puts it in his book, *Soundtracks: The Surprising Solution to Overthinking*, "true, helpful, and kind." With all of this progress, albeit slow, was some sense of clarity that was beginning to form in me about what was healthy and unhealthy about my surroundings. My radar was up now. I was journaling my thoughts, keeping lists of which ones I needed to retrain. The mistake I made in those early years of my counseling was confusing progress with a cure. When I began feeling better, I would slack off the tools that Brad had taught me and end up right back in the cycle I was in so many times before.

By this time, I had finally met with our family physician who prescribed me the norm for an adult who is experiencing depression and anxiety symptoms, Lexapro. I was prescribed 10 mg to take once a day, and within the first few days, I could tell something was physically off in my body. I felt like I had shot-gunned a six-pack of Red Bull as my nerves were the most on edge I had ever felt. I couldn't physically sit still. I quickly called the doctor's office, and they informed me that this was a common side effect for some people. Wait, what? A common side effect of anxiety meds is to make you more anxious? That didn't seem right! They explained to me that the chemical makeup of some people reacted oppositely to this particular drug. In this case, they would prescribe me with the generic version of it, escitalopram. First, I was relieved to hear there was an alternative, because I wasn't sure I could live with this stuff in my system. Second, I was glad it was a generic drug because that meant lower prescription costs.

Although my dosage has fluctuated over the years, I currently still take Escitalopram every day, but am working with my physicians to phase it out completely. It was so timely, though. Between the prescription every day and counseling sessions with Brad every other week, I was feeling better than I ever had before. My wife and kids began to notice a difference too, as they didn't have to walk on eggshells around me anymore (something that I hated I put them through as I remember having to walk on eggshells in my home growing up around both parents).

This was the penultimate resolution of my story, or so I thought. It turns out that I would have to be reminded time and time again that this is a journey, not a one-step fix.

The battle in my mind was and is ever-present. The difference is the tools that I have gained over the years, and that was a toolbox I was just beginning to fill.

A GLIMMER OF HOPE

By now it was 2017, and clarity was my new friend. I hadn't understood the power that my thoughts had over me until I began the work of retraining them—work I still continue today. We began establishing some new rhythms and life patterns in our little family and home that seemed to help too. Sarah was relieved I had someone to talk to but still offered an ear whenever I needed it, she never wavered.

As we approached the ten year mark of full-time ministry, I was due a sabbatical from the work. Our church had a plan in place that every seven years, you could receive a paid sabbatical because our pastor and elder team knew the emotional toll that local church ministry has not just on the minister, but on their whole family as well. My pastor at the time had gone twenty years without a sabbatical before 2015, when the elders decided it was way overdue. This led them to establish the practice of every seven years for full-time clergy. I was grateful because I knew that meant I would be due very soon. In 2016, we launched a huge building campaign to expand our campus and build new offices and an auditorium. For a few years now, the staff had been kicked out of their offices to make more room for kids' classrooms on Sunday mornings and Wednesday nights. So, we on staff were all eager to get this campaign rolling, even though it meant late nights and long hours.

We made it through the building campaign and construction, and as the summer of 2017 approached, the elders knew I was overdue for the sabbatical I had been promised. They paid for a house for my family and I to vacation in Charleston, South Carolina—a trip that we still talk about to this day. With my newfound journey in clarity of thought, Sarah and I used this sabbatical as a time to consider our future in central Indiana. There were lots of things keeping us there: tenure at the church, friends and relationships we had built, kids' friends, babysitters, great neighbors, a house that was half paid off by that point, and extremely low cost of living.

However, there were two very strong pushes for us to consider our time in Indiana was done. First, my parents' health was declining rapidly. It was becoming more and more evident that I would have to take the role of caretaker at some level at some point. My sister was not much help there as she was still trying to get her life straight after her time in prison. My dad was out of work now due to two bum knees he had to have replaced, one resulting in a blood clot that left him on blood thinners for the rest of his life. When he was forced into early retirement, his whole sense of self-worth came crumbling down with it. He had always drunk alcohol for as long as I could remember, but when his life shifted through an early, forced retirement, it became out of hand quickly. He abused alcohol in a way that we had never seen before: drinking himself to sleep for days at a time, wrecking his truck, taking swings at my mother, falling down, and constantly urinating himself. He would even drink mouthwash or aftershave to get as drunk as possible as quickly as possible. My mother, who was already spiraling in her mental state with a condition that we didn't know she had at the time, was getting increasingly intolerable. Calling me with every piece of bad news of bad behavior from my sister and dad. It was a lot to bear, and I couldn't have survived it if it weren't for the medication and counseling I received.

Brad counseled me about boundaries, and I tried my hardest to establish those with my ailing family back in Virginia, but it often got the best of me. I just couldn't understand why they couldn't get it together. I was, and am, a firm believer that if you're still on this earth, then you still have a purpose, a reason to be here. For the life of me, I couldn't understand what my mom's, dad's, and sister's purpose was other than to torment me from afar. I know that's a selfish and limited view, but that's how I felt. So, you can see why it was becoming increasingly more crucial to try to move closer to Virginia so that I could help my family in any way that I could as they were self-destructing.

The second reason we were strongly considering leaving was my consistent butting heads with our lead pastor and his wife. By this point, through counseling and additional reports of others experiencing the same effects of their leadership as I did, I knew that toxicity was playing a role in how I was feeling there serving under them both. To say it was a toxic environment is putting it lightly. I'd rather not go into all the details, but it was becoming more and more difficult to follow their leadership with enthusiasm.

It is for these reasons that we decided, after ten and a half years in ministry in central Indiana, that in the beginning of 2018, we would begin searching for a position at a church closer to our family in Virginia. This was a very difficult decision, one that took us almost a year to make. We hated leaving behind all the relationships and community we had built up, but we knew what we had to do.

I tried my hardest to leave in the best way possible, and though it was friendly and cordial, I was scared, unhealthy, never fully honest with my pastor about the full reasoning for us moving on. I took that job expecting to retire from that church. That's what I desired, but the story God was writing for my family seemed to be much different.

We searched for church jobs closer to but not necessarily in Virginia. We wanted to be close enough to get there at a moment's notice, but not so close we had to expose our kids to the constant drama of what was happening with my family. We had a few interviews and a few offers before we accepted what appeared to be a dream role for me at a church just south of Baltimore, Maryland. In the spring of 2018, we said our goodbyes with much fanfare to our friends, and what had become family, in central Indiana. I still miss it there; we all do.

We temporarily moved in with Sarah's aunt and uncle on the north side of Baltimore while we looked for a house we could afford on the southside near the church. This was not as easy as it seemed. We had lots on our wish list, honestly a lot of the things we had in our small home in Indiana were what we were looking for. On top of that demand, the housing market in central Maryland was about two and a half times as expensive as it was in Indiana. We outstayed our welcome in her aunt and uncle's home with our family uprooted from everything we ever knew. We settled for a small bungalow house that we made a home in Linthicum Heights, Maryland.

My role at the church was the same as I had in Indiana—creative arts pastor—but this time I had a worship leader on staff, hired at the same time as me, that I would get to lead. I was so pumped! This was going to be great! And it was great, mostly. We quickly learned, however, a couple of harsh realities: first, central Maryland was not the place for us. It was crowded, poorly kept, and full of drug addicts. It was so far out of our comfort zone that we never really felt comfortable or at peace there. It was certainly nice being that close to family in Virginia, though. Only a four-hour drive as opposed to the twelve hours it took from our home in Indiana. There were pockets of central Maryland we enjoyed. Annapolis was our go-to city to roam. Washington, DC was just a short forty-five-minute drive away, which boded well for Sarah and me, as we were lifelong Washington Redskin/Football Team/Commanders fans. I was able to attend a few games while we lived there, and it was a dream come true. We went on hikes; went to MLB games, concerts, and restaurants in DC; and went to NASCAR races in Dover, Delaware. It was a fun couple of years in that regard, but it just never felt like home.

> By now, I was realizing that my mental state was affecting my relationship with authority.

The second thing we quickly realized was that we were sold a bill of goods from a lifetime salesman turned senior pastor at the church I accepted a role at. We soon brought on Sarah to help build my team there, and when we were left alone, things were great. But I soon realized the vision of the church that I was sold on was not in fact where they were headed. We had moved away from the conservative Baptist church world when we were married in 2006 and hadn't looked back. This church though, and their pastor, seemed dead set on returning to conservative styles of ministry that did not align with my style at all. Needless to say, we butted heads, a lot. By now, I was realizing that my mental state was affecting my relationship with authority, something that one of my high school band directors noticed and called out a long time ago, but I never learned that lesson.

What I told myself after leaving Indiana was to be as honest as possible from now on with my lead pastor (boss). I carried the weight of guilt and shame for overstaying my welcome at my last church, and I wouldn't go through that again. I was going to speak my mind. Well, as you can imagine, that went over like a fart in church. I let our pastor know, frequently, that I didn't agree with where we were headed as a church, thinking that he valued my opinion enough to consider a course correction. Instead, he tried to get me to come around, and when I refused, he convinced the elders that my time there was limited. I knew it too. Towards the end of 2019, I began searching for a new church to work for, and this time I didn't care where it was. COVID-19 put a little pause in this journey, but we eventually ended up where we are today, outside of Atlanta, Georgia. (Remember, in 2007 when Sarah and I prayed for God to send us to the southeast, Georgia was one of a few states I tried to crack into but never could.)

During the pandemic, my team at the church in Maryland worked frantically to produce a church service with no audience. It was weird, but a fun challenge. By March of 2020, I was getting closer to the final stages of the interview in Georgia that was put on hold from the pandemic. One morning, we were asked to meet with the pastors and elders where they informed us that our worship leader would be fired right after that meeting with us and that we had until July to find a new place to work. We were a little surprised and extremely offended. The elders just sat there and didn't speak a word of defense for us. I got on the horn with the church in Georgia, and we solidified the deal rather quickly. By July 2020, we were living in Georgia, and I was working at a church in the west Atlanta suburbs.

Easily the best thing to come out of my time in Maryland, besides a lot of free education on what not to do in church work, was a few relationships. No matter where life has taken us, relationships have always been something we've gained and treasured greatly. Maryland was no different. One of my best friends today is Chris Comstock, who wrote the foreword to this book. Chris was the student pastor at the church in

Maryland at the time that I was hired there in 2018. He and I quickly rose to the leadership team together and grew an immediate bond with each other. We both loved what we did, loved our families, and loved to read and learn. Most importantly, we both loved to eat! Chris was actually applying to the same church in Georgia as I was for a separate role at the same time I was applying. Through a series of events only God could have orchestrated, Chris ended up there before me and was one of two influential people that got me the job there. I love Chris to death. He has been one of the most influential people in my life to date.

Along with Chris, I met Mitch Benedict. He was the worship leader they hired and fired along with me. Mitch was young and smart, and his love for people still encourages me to this day. We talk regularly, and his beautiful family is back home in Pennsylvania serving in a great church there. We met Mario and Cynthia Furst in Maryland. Cynthia was on staff as the guest services director and eventually made her way onto my team at the church in Maryland. She and her husband, Mario, are two of the most wonderfully hospitable people you'll ever meet, and we remain great friends today.

This was a lot of moving for us in a short period of time. Sarah and I never moved when we were growing up, so this was all a bit of a shock to our system, some may say trauma! Through all of it, I learned how to rely on God more than ever before this point, and our family became stronger because of it.

My wife had been feeling the urge to homeschool now for a few years. I fought it because every homeschooler I had known at that point was socially awkward and unaware of current events. Through the pandemic, we got a free test run at home schooling. As it turned out, Sarah and I both were pretty unhappy with the public school system in Maryland at that point. Our kids would come home from school not wanting to go back because of bad kids in their class doing things to distract and scare them. Our protective mode kicked into high gear. We had meetings with the teachers and principals to no avail. So, when COVID-19 hit and we got a taste of the homeschooling life, we leaned in. I had never seen Sarah so motivated before. She is an amazing mother and an incredible wife but I didn't realize how great of a teacher she was too. It didn't take long before I was convinced we could do this homeschooling thing and we wouldn't have to raise two weirdos, but rather, we would have the freedom to teach them however we saw fit as their parents. No one besides God would ever love them the way we did, and we wanted to impart that love and God's wisdom into them directly.

Sarah launched an LLC for a graphic design business when we moved to Georgia. Financially, I needed her to bring in a little bit each month so that we would have more than just the bare minimum to survive. She has been homeschooling, designing, and farming ever since we moved to our little one-acre homestead, and I wouldn't have it any other way.

CHAPTER EIGHT

LEARNING TO GRIEVE

By 2019, my mom was officially, and reluctantly, diagnosed with dementia. Although this explained a little why we had fought so endlessly for so long, the struggle was far from over. Her doctor and my counselor I was seeing at the time in Maryland had urged me to gain power of attorney over her as soon as possible, before her disease got any worse. I was hesitant to get into this, but I knew those advising me were right. So, I did what was right and got power of attorney over her and for most of my dad's rights too.

During this time, someone handed me a book called *Loving Someone Who Has Dementia: How to Find Hope While Coping with Stress and Grief* by Pauline Boss. I let it sit on my nightstand collecting dust while I became increasingly more frustrated with my mom and my inability to get through to her. During one visit, she argued with me about what day of the week it was for a solid hour while my dad sat in the corner shaking his head. Dad would call me, often, that year saying that mom needed to be put in a home and that he couldn't take care of her anymore.

I don't know if you ever really feel grown up as an adult. Even today, I know that I'm an adult because of my age and what societal responsibilities and freedoms I have, but I still feel like a kid inside, just trying to figure it out. No one fully prepares you for adulthood, at least they didn't for me. I still pick up the phone to call for help whenever I need it. I'm not immune to asking for help, but this had me feeling paralyzed with inadequacy. I didn't know how to care for crippling parents. I fought this tooth and nail because I knew my godly responsibility was in providing for and protecting my family: Sarah and the kids. I had no interest in putting my parents' needs over theirs, but honestly, that was just fear. I was afraid I couldn't do it. Afraid that I didn't have what it took. I was angry at my sister who, being six years older than me, should have been the first one in line to take care of all of this, but she could barely take care of herself and her three children. I wanted to honor my father and mother, like the Bible had taught me, but I was too afraid to do what was right. I tried to muster up the courage though and be for them what they needed, not what they wanted.

> I still feel like a kid inside, just trying to figure it out.

My mom begged me, through tears, not to put her into a home, and although I tried to many times, I never did. I feel peace about that decision to this day that I was able to honor one of her last requests. My mom was in such torment, such mental and physical pain those last few years of her life. I would break down crying throughout the day just thinking about what she was going through. It didn't seem fair.

By this point in 2019, through the power of attorney, I had sold my childhood home, which was very emotional for me. I still have storage containers full of memories I have yet to sift through, though I have begun to go through some for the purpose of writing this book. I moved my parents into an apartment complex where an amazing family from their church, the church I grew up in, would look after them almost daily. Lisa and Scott Brooks were a godsend, and I owe them everything for the way they loved my family and my parents. They had no reason to do so other than the love of God, and I pray their reward is rich because of it someday.

This brings us to the most painful part of my story. One that I have shared often while holding back tears and with lumps forming in my throat. It began in the summer of 2020 while I was down in Georgia on my final interview with Sarah at the church down here. We were borrowing a friend's minivan to cruise around different areas of town that we might look at to buy a house when my phone rang. It was dad. I had often ignored his calls when I just couldn't emotionally deal with whatever he was going to complain about, but that day, I answered. His voice was broken and a bit panicked and confused as he told me there had been a terrible car accident in which my sister, Noelle, and her daughter, Chloe, had been killed. I immediately pulled into a parking lot and tried to make sense of what was going on as I heard my mom in the background crying. I asked dad where he heard this from, as my dad at this point was diagnosed with early-onset dementia himself, and I didn't believe him. I thought, *Surely this isn't true.* He said he had received a call from Scott Brooks telling him what had happened. I told dad I would call Scott and see what was going on. My heart pounded, Sarah in the passenger seat asking what was happening, and I couldn't explain it all yet.

I got Scott on the phone, and he had no idea what I was talking about and prayed it wasn't true. So, I thanked him, called dad back, and he said he wasn't sure who it was that called, but he knew what he had been told. I don't remember much of who I called next, but I limped my way back to Chris's house, as he had already moved to Georgia, and tried to figure out what was going on. While on their front porch, I got in touch with the sheriff's office who said they were on their way over to my parents' apartment and would contact me after that. By then, my aunt, my dad's sister, was on her way to their apartment too.

It was June 27, 2020, my dad's seventieth birthday. My sister and all three of her kids were headed to the beach for the day then back for dinner with my parents for dad's birthday. They were driving on Route 460, a four-lane highway with no median that is notorious in our area for fatal accidents. At the same time, there was a high-speed pursuit happening on Interstate 295. The suspect's car exited onto Highway 460 and, shortly after, struck my sister's car head on, killing her instantly. When the sheriffs arrived at my parents' apartment, they had my aunt call me, and they told my parents while I was on the phone that my sister had in fact been killed in a car accident and that Kaitlyn, her oldest daughter, not Chloe, like we had previously thought, had also passed away after being airlifted to the hospital. Chloe and Blake, my sister's two youngest, were also injured pretty badly and were in the hospital but were expected to recover.

In an instant, our lives were changed; my parents were devastated. Their firstborn child and their firstborn grandchild were both taken from them at the same time, far too soon. I was in shock—I had no idea what to do. My heart mourned the loss of my sister and niece, but even more mourned for my parents who had lost their daughter, and for Chloe and Blake who had lost their mother and sister.

I had experienced some loss in my family by that point. Both of my grandparents had long since passed away. My Uncle Eddie, my dad's only brother and my favorite uncle, passed away from cancer in his early forties. Sarah had lost an uncle to cancer as well. But this one hit differently. This was way too close and way too sudden and way too sad. In the days that followed, I had to make all the arrangements for a funeral as my parents were unable to, and now I was the only one left. It hurt so badly to watch them hurt. My in-loves, as we call them, Billy and Tracy, Sarah's parents, along with Scott and Lisa and the church were all an amazing help during this time. I remember that my aunt had to identify the picture of my sister's body, and I was grateful my parents didn't have to but imagined what that must've looked like as by then I had known just how violent of an accident it really was. I remember Sarah and her mom cleaning off my sister's blood-covered purse so that I could go through it and get what I needed to make arrangements for her. She had no life insurance, so we decided to cremate her, and we gave the ashes to her remaining oldest daughter, Chloe. Sarah and I bought her a ring that had my sister's ashes in it so she could take her momma with her wherever she went in life. I'm so proud of Chloe, now out of high school and on her way to being a nurse, making her momma and all of us so proud. I created a video from family photos of my sister's life and watched in tears on the front row of that church with my parents on either side of me.

That was it. What was formerly a family of four—my dad, mom, sister, and me—was now a family of three. I watched helplessly as my mom's health spiraled quickly downhill. What I learned in that time was that trauma was to dementia what gasoline was to fire. My mom's falls became more frequent as her neurologist described to me that the dementia slowly, or in this case, rapidly, unplugs the wires in your brain that helps you function physically or mentally. By August of that year, my mom had taken one too many falls, and hospice was called in. Now living in Georgia, I went up to Virginia for a week shortly after that to spend as much time with her and dad as possible. Dad was still in shock, I think. He knew his only daughter was gone, and now he was watching his wife die.

Scott and Lisa to the rescue again, but not for the last time. They set up the hospice bed in a bedroom in their home and cared for my mother 24/7 the last month or so of her life. Mom could no longer feed herself and was having difficulty even swallowing. We knew the end was near. During that week I spent with her, I held her hand, sang to her some of her favorite hymns, and prayed over her. I thanked her, though she couldn't communicate with me because the dementia was so set in and because of the morphine she was on to stay comfortable and rest. I thanked her for being such a great momma and told her it was ok for her to go to heaven now. I said my goodbyes, watched as my dad spoke to her as if she would answer back, then drove back down to Georgia. The next week, I got the call that she was gone.

I had now lost my sister and my mother in less than three months. This loss was different. I had time to say goodbye. Although the dementia brought her completely down very quickly after my sister's death, I still had time to emotionally prepare. In the past handful of years leading up to this point, if you had told me that my alcoholic father who seemed dead set on drinking himself to death would outlive my mom and my sister, I wouldn't have ever believed it. But that's exactly what happened, and it happened very fast. Once again, I planned a funeral, this time speaking all that I remembered and loved about my mom to everyone in the service. Here's what I read that day at mom's funeral:

My earliest memory of mom was curling up next to her at night while she read to me The Berenstain Bears for the millionth time. The smells of Sunday's fried chicken and laundry detergent still on her chest as she rubbed my back to sleep.

I remember her dragging me to church. I knew it was the right thing to do, and so did she, though I'm not sure either of us really wanted to go.

I remember her baking countless casseroles for our family and, when dad caught wind of it, he would show up with pizza instead.

I remember playing in the sand with her during our Myrtle Beach vacations. She would sunburn like me; dad and Noelle always tanned. I remember we loved floating down the lazy river together.

I remember her being so selfless, always putting the three of us first, especially daddy. If we made a peep while dad was sleeping off the graveyard shift, we'd sure pay for it.

I remember her "going sailing" at local yard sales every Saturday she could, searching the earth for the best deals this side of the Mississippi. I grew up wearing either yard sale clothes or JCPenney store brand, as dad had a credit card there.

I remember her always celebrating with her family and friends. Never without a gift for anyone on a birthday or anniversary.

I remember our Christmas Eves on Collingwood Drive. She made more food than the county could eat, but she was proud of every ounce of it. She loved having our family over there that special night each year.

I remember how she loved the Beatles and danced to them while telling us of her youth when she used to be cool with her friends and how upset she was when the band broke up.

I remember the stories of her and dad meeting, marrying, traveling the east coast to beaches and racetracks, having their first child, my sister Noelle, and eventually me, a surprise.

I remember how much she longed to be around people and travel the road. If you could take her somewhere she'd never been and let her spend some money along the way, you won her heart.

I remember the time she caught the kitchen on fire cooking for dad and how bad she felt about it. I remember dad hanging a sign in that kitchen the next day: "Nita's Kitchen: Home of the Well-Done French Fry." She laughed.

I remember every Sunday after dragging us to church she would come home and make us the best fried chicken you've ever eaten, although she always toted it was "nothing special".

I remember her kitchen was the aroma of my childhood. Her hugs, the feeling of great pride in her family.

I remember the struggles, for sure, but boy, do I remember her laugh.

I remember how much she loved Noelle and would stop at nothing to do anything for her, despite all the heartache she put us through. She did the same for me too, but I think we all know which child was more independent.

I remember how devastated she was earlier this year when she lost her firstborn child and firstborn grandchild on the same day, my father's seventieth birthday.

I remember she had thick, short, strawberry blonde hair, just like me. I remember when she used to be taller than me.

I remember how much she loved daddy, no matter what they faced in their forty-five years of marriage. Mom always said she didn't want me to grow up in a broken home, and for her tenacity, I am forever grateful.

I remember how much she loved Jesus and took pride in how her grandmother raised her to know Him. She read her grandmother's Bible all the time.

I remember how much she loved me, and how proud she was of me. I never had to question that, as all of her friends and our family would tell me, and still do.

I remember a mother whose whole life was a struggle, but I remember how much she looked forward to the day when that struggle was over. Wednesday, September 23, she finally went home. No more struggle, only victory in Jesus.

Unfortunately, the amount of loss I experienced so closely together in time would not let up.

By early 2021, I had to move dad out of the apartment as their complex was not renewing their lease. The property manager had had enough of fire alarms going off and trash piling up outside of their apartment door. Through an old friend of my aunt, we found a split home right around the corner from Scott and Lisa for dad to live in. This was a huge blessing and yet again, Scott and Lisa stepped in to save the day and care for my father while I lived in Georgia. Dad was still drinking heavily, though not nearly as often. Although it seemed he had little to live for, he did have a weekly lunch with at least one friend and spent his days watching baseball and sitcom reruns in that tiny home. We still had to monitor his shopping because he would buy sleeping pills and swallow them like candy until he fell asleep. On one hand, I can't blame him. He went through a lot in the last few years of his life. I got up to see him as often as I could, and we talked on the phone about every other day. With him it was never a deep conversation. Always about baseball, the weather, or what the kids were up to that day. My amazing kids even made it a regular practice to call dad and talk to him. They are so wonderful, and I'm blown away by their kindness sometimes.

As we approached the one-year anniversary of my sister passing and what would have been my dad's seventy-first birthday, my kids called and spoke with him on a Tuesday in mid-June. They said he was happy to hear from them and sounded in good spirits and good health. By Thursday of that week, I tried to call him, but he didn't answer. This was unusual because dad was basically sitting at home alone most of the time waiting for the phone to ring or for someone to come visit as he had long since lost his license from all the DUI charges. After not reaching him on the first attempt, I tried again about ten minutes later, thinking maybe he was in the shower. When he still didn't answer, I began to get pretty worried and felt like something had happened. I called Scott and Lisa who said they hadn't heard from him either but would go over and check on him that evening. I called his lunch buddy, John, who also said he hadn't heard from him. I was worried he may have gotten his hands on some pills or alcohol again. John was too, so he said he would drive over there and see what was going on.

> ...that's three deaths, my whole childhood family, all gone within twelve months.

Around dinner time on June 16, 2021, I received a call that I had prepared my heart for for many, many years. I lived just about every day for the past decade ready to get a call that dad was gone, and that day had finally come. Lisa Brooks called me with tears in her voice and whimpered out that "he's gone." I asked what she meant but immediately knew he had passed away.

If you're keeping track, that's three deaths, my whole childhood family, all gone within twelve months. My sister in late June 2020, my mother in September 2020, and now my dad in mid-June 2021. Each of the losses were different. My sister was sudden and traumatic. My mom's passing was expected, and I had a chance to say goodbye.

With my dad, while it wasn't necessarily unexpected, it certainly was sudden. There were so many things I wanted to say to him like I had the chance to do with mom. My dad, despite his flaws, was still my hero in the way dads are every son's hero. And now he had gone to heaven, which I found some peace in. I, once again, for the third time in a year, planned a funeral. In the same way I honored my mom at her funeral, I honored my dad with the reading of a letter of remembrance. Here is what I read:

My earliest memory of dad was following him around the yard with my toy lawnmower while he cut the grass. I felt like such a hero of our family, and he made me feel that way.

I remember him always working hard. He worked shift work for over thirty years at what was then called Stone Container, and he made so many lifelong friends during that time. He would come home from whatever shift he was on to do more work around the yard, always keeping it looking great. That was a great joy of his.

I remember him missing some things in my childhood due to his work schedule, but when he was able to be there, he was all in.

I remember a generous dad. Christmas was his favorite time of year, and he was ALWAYS surprising us with gifts or his legendary dinners. Speaking of Christmas, Christmas Eve was his single most favorite day of the year, and he made it magical. He acted differently that day and consistently told me every year that he never wanted Christmas Eve to be over. He drew out Christmas morning as long as possible so that it wouldn't be over so fast. It used to drive my sister and I crazy because we just wanted the gifts. Dad wanted the joy of seeing his family enjoy what he worked so hard to provide.

I remember Myrtle Beach vacations, sometimes twice a year. The beach was in my dad's blood, there's no denying that. He wanted to be the first one on the beach and the last one to leave it each day we were there. We counted down the days as a family until that legendary drive down I-95 each August. It meant the end of summer to most, but it meant everything to me.

I remember his love for music. Even before I knew of his past and the joy playing music had brought to his teenage years, he would call me down from my room to listen to a song he was playing on our living room stereo and call out different instruments that were playing for me to admire. He had a stack of cassettes, 8-tracks, and records that he played constantly. If racing wasn't on TV, music was being played in our home. He passed on that love of music to me and taught me more about it than he forgot.

He loved his time playing music with his friends in high school. I've heard every story multiple times. When they reunited when I was a teenager, I never saw dad happier. It was a gift to get a glimpse into the magic they used to make in the form of music together. It was an honor to get to know many of those guys.

I remember our shared and passed-down love for NASCAR. His daddy took him to the races, and he took me. He loved it so much that he and my mom went to the World 600 in Charlotte on their honeymoon (and then off to Myrtle Beach, of course). Some of my earliest memories are in the turn-one stands of Southside Speedway, rooting on the likes of Eddie Johnson in that baby-blue Ford. The corndogs and the nighttime air filled with racing fumes meant everything with him beside me. I've since passed on that love of racing to my son and had the incredible privilege to attend a few races at Southside Speedway with my dad and my son before it closed down. It wasn't about *the racing as much as it was the shared love of something between a father and son. I'm forever grateful we had that bond.*

I remember how much he loved baseball, specifically the Yankees. I never understood fully why such a southern man would like a team from up north, but he was loyal, never wavered from team to team. His teams were his teams and that was final. He said he loved the Yankees because he grew up in the era when that team was bigger than life. He would drag a TV out of the garage near our fire pit in the backyard in October where we would watch the World Series together.

His loyalty carried over into his friendships. His friends meant so much to him, and he would speak so highly of them to me constantly, all the way up to the last time we talked.

I remember fishing trips with him and Uncle Eddie. I once fell asleep on the pier in Sandbridge on an all-night fishing trip with the two of them. Uncle Eddie woke me up with a fish in my face, asking me to kiss it. Dad laughed; so did I.

I remember how proud he was of me. He was never one to say that while I was growing up, but he confided it to my mom, and she told me of his pride every chance she got.

I remember how much he loved to laugh. Hardly ever without a joke, his laugh was infectious. We used to stay up after his 3:00 p.m. to 11:00 p.m. shifts and eat junk food and watch The Three Stooges *together.*

I remember how much the words "thank you" meant to him. Gratitude was very important to him, and he instilled this in me every chance he got. Thank you, dad, for that.

I remember how much he loved his brothers, sisters, dad, and mother. His brother was his best friend, no one came close. He loved his sister and being around her every chance he got. I watched him love his mom the way a son should when they're all grown up. I saw him honor his dad even if he didn't think he deserved it at times. I remember how heartbroken he was as he watched many of his family pass from this life to the next. This was, and still is, a lesson in love for me.

I remember how, even though he wasn't sure how to share his emotions, he loved very deeply, and it was noticeable. After growing up and leaving home, I would never leave dad's presence to go back home with my family without dad crying. Now, having a son of my own, and reflecting on the times we had together for eighteen years before I left home, I understand why he cried.

I remember a dad that was far from perfect and caused much pain in my family in the last ten to fifteen years. But I know deep down who the man really was and that he was hurting a lot. I forgave him constantly.

I remember the day I got the call that he finally made the decision to follow Jesus. He had fought it for so long, but our common love for music caused him to attend a Charles Billingsley concert while I was in Florida for my summer college internship. Charles actually led him to Christ, and I spoke with dad and Charles on the phone, and we celebrated.

I remember a dad whose whole life was a struggle, but I remember how much he persevered regardless. Wednesday, June 16, he finally went home. No more struggle, only victory in Jesus.

All of this loss lends the quick life course of How to Grieve 101. By this time, I was seeing my current counselor, Kristy, who taught me how to grieve. Due to my rocky past and sometimes uneven present, I was afraid that if I allowed myself to grieve or cry or mourn these losses then I would somehow slide into a deep depression that I would never be able to get out of. Kristy warned me of just the opposite, which made perfect sense. "If you hold all of this in, you will be more depressed and anxious than ever," she said. I knew that was true, but I was still afraid. But slowly, I let myself honor their memory by mourning the loss of them in my life on earth. Sadness is a part of life; it's a part of the journey, the growing, the living. It is not to be skipped over like a track on an album you don't particularly care for. It's like fruits and vegetables, necessary for a balanced mental state.

> "If you hold all of this in, you will be more depressed and anxious than ever."

These deaths left me feeling like an orphan, abandoned by my earthly family to figure the rest out on my own. But God knew better than that. He put people in life that encouraged me to grieve, and we all saw the healthy benefits of it.

My friend, Chris, whom I mentioned earlier, lost his brother and best friend in an unexpected accident almost identical to the one that took my sister's and niece's lives. In that accident, his brother and brother's wife passed, leaving behind three beautiful children. That accident took place just one day after my mom passed in September 2020. In an instant, we had each other to walk through grief with. His wife, Renee, had lost her sister unexpectedly in December 2019 when we were ministering in Maryland together. And here we all were, still very present in each other's lives, living in suburban Georgia together, learning how to grieve at the same time in life from losses that were too soon and too sudden.

You see, I believe in order to grieve properly, God gives us the right people at the right time. I needed Kristy to teach me how to mourn, and I needed Chris to mourn alongside. The answer to grief, even though it never goes away, is to surround yourself with the right people, allow yourself to feel sad when you need to, and talk about those you have lost on a regular basis.

My kids are really great at asking questions about my mom, dad, and sister. It's sad, yes, but I'm grateful I have those memories and that other people like Sarah, Chris, Kristy, and my kids care enough to talk about them with me.

CHAPTER NINE

SPECIAL DELIVERY

> "Every
> movement
> backwards
> creates
> momentum
> to go
> forward
> again."

There are moments in life that spur us onto the next phase or the next lesson whether we want it to or not. Some are intentional, some are mistakes. We all begin our lives thinking the proverbial arrow in our timeline as it travels from left to right will also go up and to the right. Growing, upward. Author Blaine Hogan says, *"Every movement backwards creates momentum to go forward again."* That may be the truest statement I've ever heard outside of the Bible. That's certainly what my life has felt like over the past forty years.

Throughout my transition of working for three churches in seventeen years of full-time ministry, I had grown increasingly bitter towards the organization of the Church. I began to wonder what we were doing with the smoke and the lights and the celebrity pastors, even in our own little corner of the world. I did, however, fall more in love with the people I ministered to and with more than the work itself, which is not something I could have said in my first half of my career. But I wanted greater connection, more relationships, less programming, less show.

I began to, more carefully this time, share those frustrations and pulls with those closest to me. Most didn't have an answer to the feelings. Some related to them, some didn't. Combine a feeling like there had to be something more to all of it with my lifelong tenure of not being able to control my words well, it was only a matter of time before my days in church ministry were over for a while.

At all the churches I had worked at, including the one here in Georgia, joking around was a common thing amongst the staff. This included, unfortunately, some coarse joking that shouldn't be entertained by the people of God. The kind of joking that I have tried my hardest since to distance myself from, although I am far from perfect. Although some may laugh with you, not everyone is comfortable in these settings. I made the mistake, like I often did in life, of taking that too far at the church here in Georgia. I had made coarse jokes in the presence of some people who didn't find it humorous, nor should they. The leaders asked me to consider my future there, and I knew what that meant. I chose to resign to maintain a sense of what little dignity I had left and climbed into the biggest and longest panic attack of my life. I had let my family down, my friends down. I walked away from church ministry in the Spring of 2023, vowing never to return. I committed to keeping my family a part of this church as I believed in the community and growth it was providing for all of us.

I had to work through bitterness and unforgiveness all over again. But this time was different. Through the ministry of this very church, my faith had grown deeper than ever before. As a body, we began to wake up to the spiritual battle that we are all in as Christians. I, like many, knew of this battle, but thought that we may be taking it a bit too far when we began casting out demons from people.

After prayer and biblical counsel, I learned the difference between "possessed" and "oppressed," and I had long since known what it felt like to be "depressed." I knew there was a stronger, unseen force at play here. It took me a while and some guided study to come around, but I sit here today a believer in the power and authority of Jesus and the oppression that authority can release you from. I nervously attended what is known in our church as a breaking free session with an amazing couple from out of state that came in to introduce us to this type of healing. In that session, nothing crazy happened, although I've heard some weird stories from others' experiences. They simply went through any unforgiveness or trauma that I was holding onto, or was holding onto me, and called it out of me with the power and authority of the Holy Spirit. I remember thinking, *This is crazy, I don't feel anything.* But I can tell leaving there I felt different, aware, lighter. My wife commented when I returned home that I seemed to be standing up straighter, which is ironic since it was spiritual oppression I was being released from. This special delivery was what God had brought me through, not around, had been about truth and its rightful place in my brain.

This year, my son and I read a book together by Jon Acuff called *Your New Playlist: The Student's Guide to Tapping Into the Superpower of Mindset.* In it, Jon and his two daughters walk through what it's like to retrain your brain with truth and rid it of the lies it can so easily begin to believe. This book is a culmination of this journey I've been on, and a great wake up call to my son, who I know struggles with the same mindset I did for many years. The difference is, now he has the tools. He has the truth and people in his life to remind him of it constantly.

In the book, Jon and his daughters encourage you to "take every thought captive" (2 Corinthians 10:5) and ask these three powerful questions of each thought: Is it true? Is it helpful? Is it kind? If you can't honestly answer yes to all three, then you don't give that thought any more attention, and you replace it with a thought that does meet that criteria.

This is the most simplified version of retraining your thoughts that I've ever come across and have since been sharing this simple tool with anyone that will listen. Try it yourself and see!

Now, I'm not saying that any one of these has been the answer to all my problems, including my mental health battle. I still take medicine and see a counselor and I still believe that everyone should be in therapy because there is, as Proverbs 11:14 says, "wisdom in a multitude of counselors."

> This whole journey, this whole "up and to the right" of growing upwards has been about me breaking free from the thoughts that lead to emotions that lead to behaviors that I don't want anymore.

What I was delivered from was not just a wake-up call to my own words, actions, oppression, and trauma, and not just from a career in the church; I was delivered from believing that I have to fight this battle on my own. Now, no Christian would admit to that, but we live that way every day. I did, for nearly forty years!

This whole journey, this whole "up and to the right" of growing upwards has been about me breaking free from the thoughts that lead to emotions that lead to behaviors that I don't want anymore.

Through medicine, therapy, and the Lord, I have found that. I am more self-aware and more filled with truth now than I have ever been. I am practicing reprogramming my neural pathways each day. I'm teaching this to my kids and anyone else who will listen. My journey of growing upward is now in people and presence.

I surround myself with friends that stretch me in areas of health, profession, faith, and finances. I call them my "board of directors" (just like Annie F. Downs). I practice being present every morning through morning pages, a practice introduced by Julia Cameron in *The Artist's Way: A Spiritual Path to Higher Creativity*. Now, when I find myself beginning to feel anxious about any unknowns of the future, I remember that God has called me to live today to its fullest, nothing more, nothing less. I remind myself of what is true, helpful, and kind. I remember that today we have everything we need, and God has never let us down before, and He never will.

As you can tell, my faith has had a major impact on my journey. I'm not here to preach to you, but I'll let you know, "the peace of God that surpasses all understanding" (Philippians 4:7) is very real.

In my next forty years, I want to exponentially grow upward, and I believe now more than ever that it's possible.

113

AFTERWORD

I believe that living free from the oppression of depression and anxiety is possible. It is a journey, a daily battle that you must be willing to show up for. I know it sucks sometimes but ignoring it will only make it worse. Again, I am not a licensed mental health expert, but I have been through these things written here and have come out stronger on the other side.

You are not alone in this, and you matter. These are not just cliches, it's the truth, and the truth really can set you free.

If you need someone to talk to, you can reach out to me at dp@dustinpead.com, and I'd be happy to lend an ear and a heart of someone who has been through it. You too can grow upward.

ACKNOWLEDGMENTS

Thank you to . . .

My wife, Sarah, who is my partner in this journey of life and growing upward.

My kids, Ethan and Aubrey, for loving me and keeping me grounded in the present.

Billy and Tracy Williamson for supporting, loving, and believing in me and our family like no one else.

Mom, Dad, and Noelle. I love you and miss you.

Nick and Lauren Williamson for loving us and keeping us tied to family and adventure.

(Aunt) Betty Sue Angle for not only her help in remembering some details for the early part of this book, but for being my favorite aunt.

Chris Comstock for being the brother I never had.

Blake Behr and Conrad Morgan for being supporters and friends beyond what I deserve.

Nick and Jamie Hampton for legitimately being family to us, always.

Brad Dobson and Kristy Mycroft for countless hours of counseling and sound biblical wisdom.

Darren Cooper for believing in me and what I have left to offer.

Omer Redden for teaching me how to write a book.

Rick Detraz for being in my corner and being someone I am honored to look up to.

Seth and Amia Freeman for being on my prayer team and genuinely some of the best humans I've ever known.

Aaron Beaver for always encouraging me to believe the best.

Blake Rackley for supporting me since college and spurring me on in this writing.

Billy and Lisa Rackely for investing so much time into my teenage years.

Scott and Lisa Brooks for loving and serving my family through the hardest years of our lives.

Caleb Campbell for being an example of chasing dreams.

Will Dogget for encouraging me to work hard and trust God.

Stephen & Jackie Brewster for being there when I need you.

Blaine Hogan for inspiring me to write this book.

Wendy and The Lost Boys for loving me all over this country.

The A.E. Williams Editorial team for taking this book to the next level of excellence.